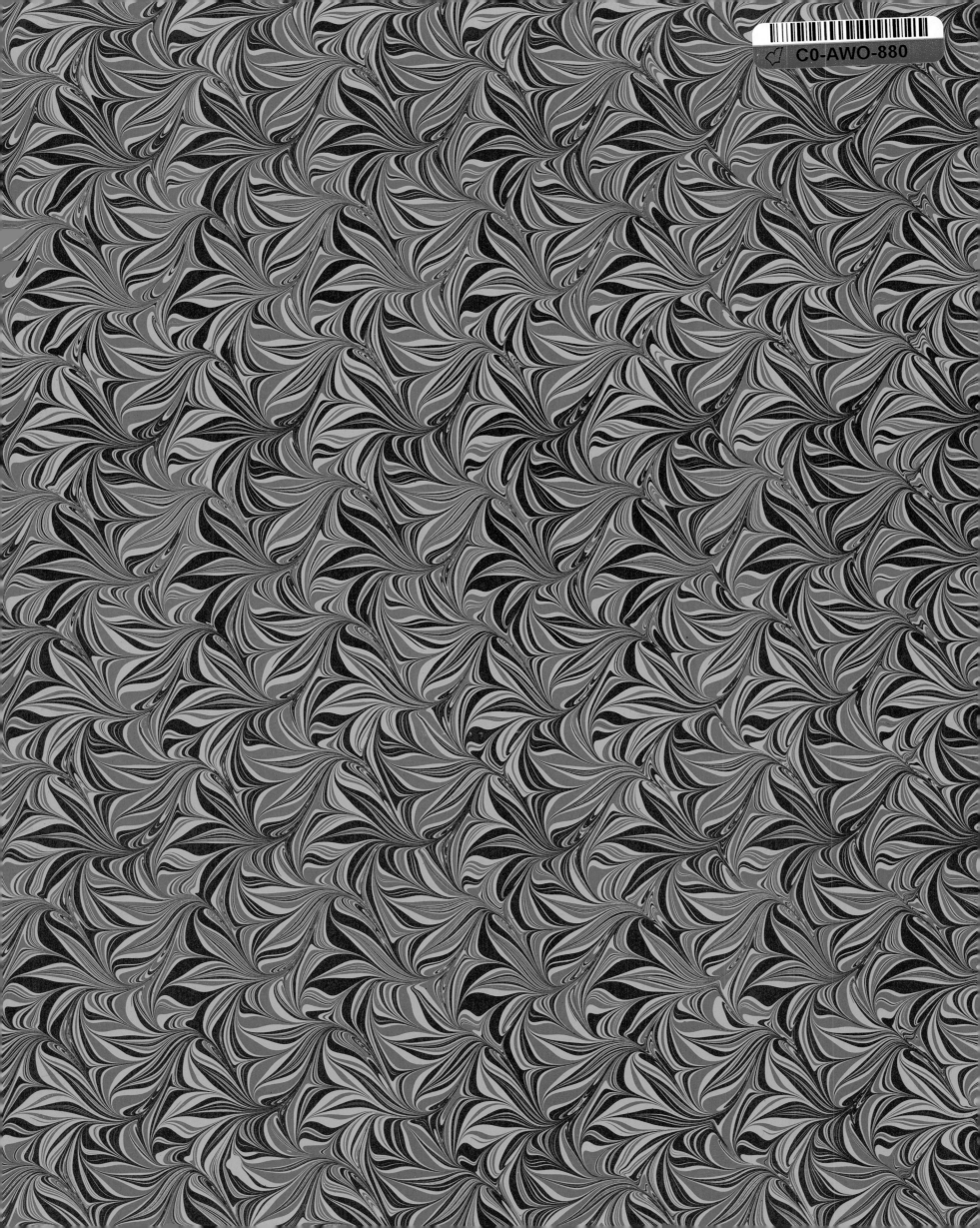

THE ORIGINAL
WATER-COLOR PAINTINGS

by

JOHN JAMES
AUDUBON

for

THE BIRDS OF AMERICA

VOLUME I

Figure 4

Figure 5

The hawk above, attributed to the Japanese painter Kano Tsunenobu, displays the same vitality as Audubon's painting of the eagle at right.

thology." And the Duc d'Orléans, who had himself traveled along the borderlands of America during a brief exile and who was to become the "citizen king" of France in the July Revolution of 1830, remarked that the pictures shown to him surpassed anything he had ever seen. Audubon was quickly elected to a number of learned societies on both sides of the Atlantic. By the time his first folios were issued he was, as the title page announced, "Fellow of the Royal Societies of London & Edinburgh and of the Linnaean & Zoological Societies of London; Member of the Natural History Society of Paris, of the Lyceum of New York, &c. &c. &c." On the title pages of subsequent editions the list of honors more than doubled in length.

This was, to be sure, a romantic age—an age when men looked to nature more eagerly and more lovingly than they ever had for evidence of the sublime designs of creation. Stepping into the social and scholarly circles of Europe with his natural lore and with the freshness of the wilderness still upon him, Audubon was a man for the times. Yet there is little reason to challenge those early estimates of his achievement. And there was certainly nothing fortuitous about his success. Only a man of his prodigious energies and his unconquerable determination could have accomplished what he did in the years he devoted to his task—a task that he felt, with almost mystical reverence, had been "allotted him by nature."

No other man of his day was so familiar with the living presence of birds. His interest in their habits and in their countless varieties mounted over the years from his childhood until it became a commanding obsession. He came to believe with passionate conviction that in the years to come no one would have the same opportunity to study the birds of America in their primeval haunts, and this realization drove him mercilessly on his quest.

He roamed the woods, the swamps, and the coasts of his adopted land with all the freedom of the wild creatures he stalked. He saw sights that have all but vanished from the American scene—and some that have gone forever: flights of great white whooping cranes majestically winging their way down to the Gulf Coast from their summer stay in Canada; ivory-billed woodpeckers, largest and mightiest axemen of their tribe, chopping the bark from trees to get at grubs and piercing the forests with their clarinetlike calls; colorful flocks of chattering parakeets; and passenger pigeons in such astronomical numbers that they

Figure 6

During November of 1820, while Audubon was making his way by flatboat down the Ohio River toward New Orleans, he recorded numerous notes on the birds he observed. One entry in his journal for 1820 included this marginal sketch of a loon.

literally blackened the sky in their flight for day after day, filled the air with the deafening thunder of their wings, and, when they stopped to perch, broke the limbs of stout trees with their accumulated weight.

He also saw the more common birds that still frequent our city streets and backyards, our suburbs, our coastlands, and our diminishing countryside—the robins and sparrows, the crows and gulls. He watched them in all their moods and pursuits. As Stephen Vincent Benét has written, Audubon lived to look at birds in all their natural freedom—darting in pursuit of tiny insects, arguing and scolding among themselves, grubbing for larvae in dead trees, taut with panic before their natural enemies, pouncing upon their prey, or tranquilly perched amid the leaves and flowers of their normal habitat. It was this fund of observation that informs and gives living spirit even to those drawings he most labored over, no less than to the quick, casual sketches in the margins of his journals (see Figure 6). We continue to look at birds as Audubon taught us to look at them.

Audubon was fully aware of the unique importance of his accomplishment. He hoped to share his vision and its realization with the rest of mankind, to reach a much wider audience than might ever see his original paintings. And it was with this idea, more than a century and a quarter ago, that he commissioned copies to be made—for the most part by the English engraver Robert Havell, Jr.—for publication in his monumental double-elephant folios of prints.

In his hope of winning a larger public, he succeeded to a degree and in ways that he could hardly have imagined. Over the years since they were first printed, it is the engraved copies rather than the artist's own paintings that have become celebrated as "Audubon originals," and that have, by and large, established his reputation. They are, on the whole, superb engravings that have become rarities themselves. Probably no more than two hundred complete sets were issued, and small wonder, since they were offered and sold at one thousand dollars a set, a staggering figure if we consider that the purchasing power of the dollar was then many, many times greater than it is today. Even Nathan M. Rothschild, with his incalculable fortune, thought the price steep and only reluctantly subscribed. Daniel Webster signed up, but it took Audubon several years of relentless badgering to exact payments from him.

Havell's prints were the same size as the drawings, each of the folios measuring 29½ by 39½ inches (untrimmed). Presumably the drawings were traced off onto copper plates; when the engraving was completed in black and white—by a combination of aquatint, etching, and other processes—colors were painted in by hand by a staff that at one time numbered fifty men and women. However, the outlines do not in every case correspond to the drawings, and in the hands of different workmen the colors were not always uniform. Audubon was dismayed by irregularities that sometimes crept into the engraving and coloring when he was not present in London to supervise the work. On one occasion he complained of the daubings of one of the hand colorists, and the whole crew quit on the spot and had to be replaced. Again, later, he wrote Havell that if more defective copies turned up he would abandon the whole project and, as he put it, "return to my own Woods until I leave this World for a better one." In 1833 he wrote his son from New York, with abiding concern but with less exasperation, "I hope to God that Havell will engrave all the Work as well as the last 2 Numbers I have seen here Nos 32 & No 33.—and that the Volumes will be coloured as well as those Numbers." Over the years, surviving copies have often faded or been disfigured by neglect and mishandling. In any case, these large prints have remained the closest approximation of Audubon's original work and have been valued accordingly. (In the winter of 1964–65 a set was sold for £23,000, or about $65,000, and certain individual engravings sell for more than the original price for all the 435 prints that were included in *The Birds of America*.) Subsequent reproductions of Audubon's birds, starting with an edition in reduced size by Audubon himself, have been for the most part copies of such copies or, indeed, copies of copies of such copies in an almost endless descent, until we lose all sight of the essential qualities of the man's original art.

The main story of Audubon's life is in his work; as a contemporary critic observed, "the work is full of the man." There is little need here for a detailed account of his earlier years; the story has been told often enough, and although there never was a time when he was not preoccupied by the study of nature, his great period of creative activity started only after his life was more than half spent. Until he was thirty-five years old, his mature career followed a relatively aimless and unproductive course which may be quickly traced.

Figure 7

These two grebes were drawn early in Audubon's career, probably during the time that the artist was in France in 1805.

He was born in what is now Haiti on April 26, 1785, the bastard son of a French sea captain and a sometime chambermaid, Jeanne Rabine, who died that same year. Four years later Captain Audubon quit his island estate. Subsequently he returned to France and to his lawful wife. She accepted her husband's youngster with motherly affection. He was given an adequate education, encouraged in his nature studies, and in due course he was legally adopted and properly baptized, with the name of Jean Jacques Fougère Audubon.

Years later, in outlining the story of his life, Audubon recalled that even when he was a little lad he had "felt an intimacy with nature bordering on frenzy"; that he had often played hooky from school to roam the fields near his home in France to search for birds' nests and eggs, lichens and flowers; and that when he was in his teens he started a series of bird drawings which at their best, he confessed, were "all bad enough" and which he burned in his dismay. Judging from what survives of his early efforts, Audubon's was obviously not a precociously gifted talent; he enjoyed no sustained training, and he mastered the problems he set himself largely by doggedly struggling with them on his own terms.

On several occasions Audubon stated that he had received formal art instruction as a youth in the studios of Jacques Louis David, who had had Louis XVI for a patron and who became the virtual dictator of French art during the days of the Directory and of Napoleon's empire. There is little reason to doubt his statements, although the training must have been brief and his earliest surviving drawings—simple profiles of birds and animals, made when he was turning twenty, still show little sophistication (see Figure 7). It took almost twenty more years of plodding effort and self-criticism before he began to draw birds in a way that satisfied him. Even thereafter he continued to revise and replace everything that he felt left room for improvement, until finally he had to leave well enough alone if he was ever to complete his published record.

In 1803, probably to avoid his conscription in Napoleon's swelling armies, Jean Jacques —or La Forest as he sometimes chose to call himself—was shipped off to America to Mill Grove, an estate near Philadelphia his father had acquired during his earlier days in the New World. Within five years he had married his English-born neighbor Lucy Bakewell and moved west to Kentucky, where he engaged in trade, bought slaves, speculated in real

Figure 8

Figure 9

The portraits of James Berthoud and his wife, at left, were probably drawn in Kentucky sometime late in 1819.

estate, and started a family. Had he prospered, he might have remained unnoticed and unremembered among the countless early immigrants who found their fortunes in the West. But his successes as a merchant were intermittent, and in the panic of 1819 he went bankrupt and was jailed. His days in trade were over, but his life's work would now begin in earnest. In the end his failure in business seems to have been providential.

When he was released from jail, penniless and desperate, he turned to his artistic talent, undertaking to make chalk portraits of his friends and neighbors for as much as five dollars a head (see Figures 8 and 9). There is no evidence that he had had practice in portraiture, but the demand for these efforts was sufficient for him to meet his immediate emergency. (Once a dead child was disinterred so that Audubon could record his likeness, which, the artist recalled, "I gave to the parents as if still alive, to their intense satisfaction.") When the local market for such commissions was exhausted, Audubon moved with his family to Cincinnati where for seven months he provided for his wife and two growing boys, Victor Gifford and John Woodhouse Audubon, by teaching drawing and French, by drawing further portraits, and by assisting in various capacities at the Western Museum, a newly founded institution devoted principally to natural history.

These passing seasons of 1819 and 1820 were of critical importance in Audubon's life. Since his arrival in America as an insouciant, somewhat dandified youth of eighteen, through the bitter experience of bankruptcy sixteen years later, he had drawn birds intermittently. Enough of those early efforts survive to indicate that at their best none of them approached the accomplishments of his later years. Indeed, almost all of them were scrapped when he finally selected his finest examples for the engravings of *The Birds of America*. For the most part stiff profiles in static poses (see Figure 10), they give only occasional suggestions of the dynamic compositions, the rich textures, and the enchanting patterns of the works he ultimately chose for publication.

Nevertheless, Audubon had learned a great deal in those years. It was during his first months in America that he performed one of the earliest, if not the first, experiments in birdbanding, to help him study the homing instinct of the phoebes that nested each spring in the caves bordering the Perkiomen Creek. And it was only shortly thereafter that he

Figure 10

Audubon drew the hawk above at the end of November, 1809.

devised a technique of wiring freshly killed birds in lifelike positions against a firm base, so that with mechanical dividers he could quickly transcribe their life-sized outlines in pencil.

During the winter of 1806–7, while working as an apprentice clerk in New York City, he had practiced taxidermy under the guidance of Dr. Samuel Latham Mitchill, then a United States Senator and later founder and first president of the Lyceum of Natural History. At that time Audubon was already shipping seeds, plants, birds, and other natural curiosities to correspondents abroad; over the years to come such transactions served not only to provide him with a helpful income but to keep him in touch with a wide community of amateur and professional natural scientists. One letter of transmittal written to his father from New York in 1807 concluded plaintively, "I wish thou would wrights to me ofnor and longuely . . . *j'espère que tu pourra lire—adieu—adieu.*" Later in life Audubon wrote numerous essays in English which—as edited, at least—are classics of American naturalist literature. But he had a long struggle with his acquired language before he could master it.

During the early years of their married life, in letters to her family and friends, Lucy occasionally mentions landscapes drawn by her "Mr. Audubon"; but none of these sketches have survived, and there is little way of judging what his competence may then have been in this genre. Very few of his known bird portraits up to this time were placed against landscape backgrounds. However, when the Western Museum was opened in June, 1820, it was reported with satisfaction by the president of Cincinnati College that the cases in which this "unrivalled collection" of wildlife was mounted had been "beautifully ornamented with appropriate landscape scenery by Mr. J. J. Audubon, executed partly in crayons and partly in water colours." As a further tribute to Audubon's skilled help in the museum's opening presentation, the report continues, "This gentleman, formerly from Paris, is professionally acquainted with the preservation of fishes and reptiles, and has prepared for the museum several specimens of both, in a manner that cannot easily be surpassed."

The force of circumstances during the months following his bankruptcy had in fact converted Audubon from an amateur to a professional artist; and with the more assiduous application required of his talents, his drawings improved measurably (see Figure 11)— along with his self-confidence and determination. In Cincinnati for the first time in his

Figure 11

Audubon's portrait of General William A. Lytle was probably done in Cincinnati during the fall of 1820.

life his work was exposed to public criticism—criticism more exacting than he had received either from his Kentucky neighbors or, earlier, from his family and friends. Cincinnati was indeed but a small backwater of the large world he might hope to conquer, but the encouragement Audubon received there undoubtedly prodded him into making the big decision in his life.

Shortly after the bird drawings he had then accumulated were shown at the museum early in 1820, the *Cincinnati Inquisitor Advertiser* reported that "the style & execution of these paintings . . . are so very superior, that we believe we hazard nothing in saying, there have been no exhibitions west of the mountains which can compare with them. Good judges have indeed declared they excell all other similar works in the United States." By the early autumn of that same year Audubon had left his jobs in Cincinnati—he had opened a drawing school there, among other things—and, leaving his family behind, had set out in pursuit of a dream that would take him almost a score of years to realize. The following spring Lucy wrote to a relative that her husband was in Louisiana "prosecuting a large work on Ornithology which when compleat he means to take to Europe to be published. The birds are all drawn from nature the natural size and embelished with plants, trees or views as best suits the purpose. It is his intention to go first to England, and I hope it will be in my power to accompany him. . . ."

What possessed the man, beyond midway in life and virtually penniless, to undertake the mammoth task of faithfully recording and publishing the untold variety of North American bird life? In spite of the good press he had enjoyed in Cincinnati, his technique in drawing still did not approach the ultimate standards he set for himself—albeit he was probably not yet aware of his capacity for self-improvement. In Philadelphia, the Scottish immigrant artist Alexander Wilson had already published several volumes of his *American Ornithology*, which in its thoroughness and authority seemed to defy competition. Audubon had met Wilson earlier in Kentucky. He had compared his drawings with the Scotsman's and was then pleased enough with the relative merits of his own works; but he must also have realized that Wilson's understanding of ornithology far exceeded his own.

Indeed, Audubon had but a rudimentary grasp of the science; he was still largely ignorant of the standard literature on the subject, and during his most intensive field work he had access to but a small part of it. Of Wilson's work, to be sure, he was keenly aware; it was both a guide and a challenge that over the years he had frequent good reasons to remember. (It was Wilson's enthusiastic supporters who were to prove Audubon's most vicious critics.) But for the rest he relied largely on his own observations; he did his own research; and he learned to draw the way he wished to draw principally by repeated efforts to improve on his own past performances.

Audubon took off on his venture with little enough ceremony. On October 12, 1820, he stepped aboard a flatboat as a working passenger, with his drawing materials, his gun, the clothes on his back, and very little else—a flute, possibly an old English translation of Linnaeus' *Systema naturae* (apparently the only reference book he carried with him), and a letter of recommendation from Henry Clay, then Speaker of the House of Representatives. In a covering letter Clay had written Audubon, "Will it not be well for you before you commit yourself to any great Expense in the preparation and publication of your Contemplated Work to ascertain the success which attended a similar undertaking of Mr. Wilson?" —a cautionary note that probably only got Audubon's back up. He was already determined to surpass anything Wilson had done, come what might. Audubon was accompanied by his thirteen-year-old protégé, Joseph Mason, a pupil who had a precocious talent for drawing flowers and plant life and who remained Audubon's daily companion and collaborator throughout most of the next two years.

Nevertheless, it was an auspicious beginning. On the long, slow passage down the Mississippi Audubon saw birds he had never seen before, and some none of us are privileged to see any more. The great Mississippi Valley offers the broadest and most tempting flyway in the world for migrating birds. From the Arctic barrens to the grassy plains of Patagonia, feathered migrants are funneled through this immense corridor in countless numbers and endless varieties—many of them en route to winter retreats in the lush green world of the Deep South. Audubon's journal brims with reports of his daily adventures as the cumbersome ark drifted downstream. One day he spied and winged a hermit thrush—somewhat surprisingly, the first he had ever seen; he puzzled over flights of "mysterious" birds he could not yet identify as cormorants (Linnaeus did not describe this American species); and he thrilled with every discovery he believed Wilson to have missed. And so on, through the passing Indian summer, the fall, and into the winter, until he docked at New Orleans in the first week of the new year of 1821, without money for a night's lodging and "with a bad head hake occasioned by drinking some Wine."

For most of the next six years Audubon kept his roving headquarters in and about New Orleans. He found the magnificent woodlands of lower Louisiana, which may still be seen there, an ornithological wonderland he remembered vividly all his life. He made a living as he could—drawing portraits; teaching drawing, French, music, dancing, and fencing; occasionally painting shop signs or murals for steamboats. It was from hand to mouth often enough. At times he added to the support of his family; at others Lucy remained the principal breadwinner by tutoring and teaching on her own account. Regardless of the vicissitudes he faced, however, Audubon stubbornly proceeded with his essential work; and it was during these years that he developed his talent within reach of his own demanding expectations. When Lucy joined him in the South in 1821 after a fourteen-month separation, he found his earlier drawings that she brought with her hopelessly inferior to what he could now produce. They were hardly adequate for the publication he had ever more fixedly in mind, and he "formed the resolution to redraw the whole of them."

Audubon continued to use the practices he had developed as a young man. "The many foreshortenings unavoidable in groups like these," he wrote a friend in later years, "have been rendered attainable by means of squares of equal dimensions affixed both on my paper and immediately behind the subjects before me." (All Audubon's birds—soaring gulls and running sandpipers—are represented as seen from eye level.) "I have *never* drawn from a stuffed specimen . . . " he added, "nature *must* be seen first alive, and well studied before attempts are made at representing it." Under the pressure of circumstances he was ultimately obliged to draw subjects from stuffed models and from skins, but these were exceptional rather than typical instances. His fond dream of visiting the farther west to study its birds did not materialize, and the subjects native to that area which he included in *The Birds of America* were drawn from skins he acquired from fellow ornithologists.

later he engaged Lehman to assist in the drawings made in Florida and in Charleston, South Carolina. During that southern trip, Lehman worked on about thirty drawings. He also completed a few water colors of birds for Audubon. His most popular contribution is undoubtedly the landscape background for the snowy egret (Plate 48). Lehman's work, like Mason's, was more opaque than Audubon's, although he rendered his plants in less detail and with a good deal more freedom and skill than Mason.

When Audubon and Lehman visited Charleston late in 1831, they met the Reverend John Bachman and his sister-in-law (later his second wife), Maria Martin, then only thirty-five years old. Miss Martin, who had made water-color sketches of plants even before meeting Audubon, soon learned how to imitate his style in painting birds and, in March of 1832, while Audubon was visiting Bachman, she made what was probably the first of several water-color copies of his work. In July of that same year, Bachman wrote Audubon that Miss Martin had drawn three plants for the artist (one of them the trumpet-creeper in Plate 193). Thereafter she worked at a number of water colors of plants and insects for Audubon, especially in the winters of 1833–34 and 1836–37, when Audubon and his younger son, John Woodhouse, visited with the Reverend Bachman. In all, Miss Martin assisted in about twenty of the drawings. Her technique was less detailed than Mason's, less skilled than Lehman's, and she was inclined to labor over her work.

Both of Audubon's sons assisted their father. On April 20, 1833, Audubon wrote to Havell, "My Youngest Son *draws Well*—Can you tell what is his or mine's work in the last Drawings you saw?" Audubon credited John with the drawings of ten birds (the American bittern, Plate 371, is one example), and Victor apparently painted oil backgrounds for about ten of the plates in *The Birds of America*. Both sons became estab-

lished artists in their own right, quite apart from their work for their father.

Audubon used a wide range of techniques to obtain his results; indeed, the techniques are so varied, and so successfully merged in the end product, that the terms "drawing" and "painting" are used interchangeably in this edition. The earliest extant Audubon drawings were done when he visited France in 1805. At that time he drew the bird first in pencil, then colored it with pastel, or colored chalk. After 1810 he occasionally painted the bills, eyes, and feet of birds in water color, and he often used water color to depict the birds' habitats. In 1821 he began a very limited use of water color to render the feathers of birds. Only a small percentage of those drawings done before 1822 were engraved by Havell and most of these were improved, or redrawn, or cut out and pasted down on a later drawing. By 1824, Audubon painted birds basically in water color; but where necessary he applied pastel over water color to simulate downy feathers, used ink, oil, and egg white to capture the gleaming surface of a bird's eye or beak, and even scratched the surface of his paper to achieve certain effects.

Knowledge of the gradual changes in Audubon's varied techniques sometimes helps the dating of his works. Almost all the drawings were done on Whatman paper, the watermark of which contains the year the paper was made, and it has been possible to determine some dates on that basis (although Audubon occasionally cut up the paper and used a piece that did not bear the watermark). He often inscribed his works with a date and place, particularly before early 1822. And, in his journals, letters, and in the *Ornithological Biography*, written to accompany the plates, he frequently notes a date and place for his drawing. Knowledge of the range of a bird or a plant, set against the dates Audubon traveled to a certain locale, has assisted in the dating. The dates which Havell noted on his engravings and the catalogue of Audubon's

works exhibited at Edinburgh in 1826 have also been of assistance. Nonetheless, a great number of Audubon's paintings have little or no definitive evidence with respect to dating; and, indeed, in some instances the date Audubon inscribed on a drawing will conflict with the date he gives in his writings—partly, no doubt, because he often wrote from memory without consulting his drawings. Wherever concrete evidence of the date of any drawing has not been available, the work has been dated on the basis of style and does not represent an absolute judgment, by any means.

Until early 1822 Audubon often inscribed a drawing first in pencil and later in ink. Although he usually erased the penciled inscription, a few of them remain—most of them partially erased, or, often, so faintly written as to be visible only upon a close examination of the original. In the text accompanying these plates, the decipherable inscriptions have been explained where they are not clearly visible. At least one hand other than Audubon's is clearly distinguishable in these inscriptions: most of the plants painted by Maria Martin are identified in her handwriting.

Audubon's skill as an artist has eclipsed —it is in appropriate perspective, to be sure—his art as a writer of natural history. He was, however, with the talented editorial assistance of William MacGillivray, one of America's most passionate and vivid nature writers. In the words accompanying these plates, his five-volume *Ornithological Biography* has been quoted liberally. All quotations from this work (and, where noted, from his journals and correspondence) are reproduced without change in syntax, spelling, or punctuation. The passages from Volume I are taken from the 1831 American reprint; the passages from Volumes II-V are from the original editions published in Edinburgh during the years 1834–39. In this edition the volumes of the *Ornithological Biography* are cited throughout as the "text."

THE PLATES
(1-223)

PLATE 1

WILD TURKEY
(Meleagris gallopavo)

"The great size and beauty of the Wild Turkey," Audubon wrote, "its value as a delicate and highly prized article of food, and the circumstance of its being the origin of the domestic race now generally dispersed over both continents, render it one of the most interesting of the birds indigenous to the United States of America." Audubon was not the first to praise the majestic fowl; Benjamin Franklin once said that he wished the turkey, "withal a true original Native of America," had been chosen as America's national symbol rather than the eagle, "a Bird of bad moral Character." Audubon assigned the wild turkey the place of honor at the beginning of his *Birds of America*. The painting was probably done in 1825 while the artist was staying at Beech Woods Plantation in West Feliciana Parish, Louisiana. It shows the male, the "great American cock," striding through cane (*Arundinaria gigantea* or *Arundinaria tecta*) characteristic of the riverbanks and swamps of the south central and southeastern United States.

Havell I

PLATE 2

BALD EAGLE
(Haliaeetus leucocephalus)

On his flatboat trip down the Mississippi in 1820 Audubon sighted this
bald eagle, or "white-headed eagle *Falco leucocephalus*" as he called it,
near Little Prairie, Missouri, and shot the bird at a distance of about one
hundred and fifty yards. "The figure of this noble bird," Audubon wrote
delightedly, "is well known throughout the civilized world, emblazoned
as it is on our national standard, which waves in the breeze of every clime,
bearing to distant lands the remembrance of a great people living in a
state of peaceful freedom." Audubon worked for four days to complete a
drawing of the eagle feeding on a Canada goose. Eight years later in England, dissatisfied with the results, he made this water-color copy of the
eagle, replacing the goose with a catfish copied from another early drawing.
A good number of these birds survive today, yet the species is now found
principally in Florida and in Alaska. Pursued by hunters and plagued by
a declining birth rate, it may, indeed, disappear from the country of which
it has long been the symbol.   Havell XXXI

PLATE 3

WHITE-CROWNED PIGEON

(Columba leucocephala)

"I saw them as they approached the shore," Audubon wrote, "skimming along the surface of the waters, flying with great rapidity, much in the manner of the common house species, but not near each other like the Passenger Pigeon. On nearing the land, they rose to the height of about a hundred yards, surveyed the country in large circles, then with less velocity gradually descended, and alighted in the thickest parts of the mangroves and other low trees. None of them could be easily seen in those dark retreats, and we were obliged to force them out, in order to shoot them, which we did at this time on the wing." Audubon painted these pigeons at Indian Key, Florida, in April, 1832, just after the birds had arrived from Cuba. His assistant George Lehman painted the flowering limb of the geiger-tree *(Cordia sebestena)*, a West Indian shrub found in the Florida Keys. Havell CLXXVII

PLATE 4

HOUSE WREN
(*Troglodytes aedon*)

When Audubon and his wife were in Pennsylvania in 1812, the artist made a pastel drawing of a male house wren. Years later, perhaps in 1824, he used the early work as a basis for the bird perched on the old felt hat in this pastel and water-color rendering. Audubon's penciled outline of the tree limb was completed by Robert Havell, Jr., in his engraving. Audubon wrote of this painting: "I knew of one [nest] in the pocket of an old broken-down carriage, and many in such an old hat as you see represented in the plate . . . I hope you will . . . look at the little creatures anxiously peeping out or hanging to the side of the hat, to meet their mother; which has just arrived with a spider, whilst the male is on the lookout, ready to interpose should any intruder come near."   Havell LXXXIII

PLATE 5 (*overleaf*)

WILD TURKEY
(*Meleagris gallopavo*)

Among the drawings Audubon made during his trip down the Mississippi in the autumn of 1820 was a pastel of a wild turkey hen (her mate appears in Plate 1). Some time later, using water color, he added the sprightly brood of chicks, and, later still, he used oil paints to fill in the habitat. This is one of only a few examples that combine the three mediums. The hen, Audubon wrote, is "leading her young progeny, with measured step and watchful eye, through the intricacies of the forest. The chickens, still covered with down, are running among her feet in pursuit of insects. One is picking its sprouting plumelets, while another is ridding itself of a tick which has fastened upon its little wing."   Havell VI

No 17. Plate 83.

House Wren. Male 1. F. 2. Young 3. 4. 5.

PLATE 6

CANADA WARBLER
(Wilsonia canadensis)

While Audubon and Joseph Mason were wandering through a Louisiana cypress swamp on August 13, 1821, Audubon shot and wounded what he believed to be a bird of an unknown species. He first gave it the name "Cypress Swamp Fly Catcher," as inscribed on the drawing, but later he renamed it "Bonaparte's Fly-catcher" in honor of Napoleon's nephew Charles Lucien Bonaparte, a naturalist whom Audubon met in Philadelphia in 1824. Actually, the bird is a young female Canada warbler. Although the painting is inscribed "Bayou Sarah Octr 5th 1821," it apparently was made the same day the bird was captured, while it was, as Audubon said, "alive and full of spirit." Mason drew the leaves and ripe seed pod of the southern magnolia *(Magnolia grandiflora)*.   Havell V

Cypress Swamp Fly Catcher Male.
Muscicapa

Drawn from Nature by John J. Audubon
Bayou Sarah Oct 5th 1821.

PLATE 9

CEDAR WAXWING
(Bombycilla cedrorum)

Audubon drew this pair of cedar waxwings at Cincinnati, as the inscription indicates, on April 11, 1820, using a combination of pencil, pastel, and water color. He observed that various plants provide these birds "with plenty of berries and fruits, on which they fatten, and become so tender and juicy as to be sought by every epicure for the table." He had "known an instance of a basketful of these little birds having been forwarded to New Orleans as a Christmas present." They never arrived, and "it was afterwards discovered that the steward of the steamer, in which they were shipped, made pies of them for the benefit of the passengers." Audubon rendered this branch of the red cedar *(Juniperus virginiana)* in water color; its "berries" are actually fleshy cones that provide one of the flavoring ingredients of gin.   Havell XLIII

PLATE 10

PARULA WARBLER
(Parula americana)

In his journal for March 26, 1821, Audubon wrote that his assistant, Joseph Mason, had killed a male "Blue Yellow Back Warbler." As inscribed, on the following day Audubon painted the male warbler and his mate, who is intently eyeing an inchworm. The flower stem can be seen through the male's body, indicating that, contrary to the usual practice, the plant was done first. Mason claimed that Audubon penciled in, and later erased, acknowledgments of his young assistant's numerous plant drawings. This red, or copper, iris *(Iris fulva)* is one of the two examples in which Audubon's credit to Mason remains. Havell XV

Blue Yellow Back Warbler. N.º 1 male. N.º 2 female.
Sylvia Pusilla

Drawn from nature by John J. Audubon
March 27.th 1831   Engd by Eggle Major

No 17.
Plate 85.   Yellow Throat Warbler. *Male*
          Sylvia ~~flavicollis~~ pensilis
               Castanea pumila
                Vulgo Chink-apin

Drawn from Nature by John J. Audubon
Louisiana Augt 1821.   F.R.S.-L.S.

PLATE 16

MAGNIFICENT FRIGATEBIRD

(Fregata magnificens)

Audubon painted this agile frigatebird (a species whose wing span reaches seven to eight feet) in the spring of 1832 in the Florida Keys. "I have given a figure of a very beautiful old male in spring plumage," Audubon wrote, "which was selected from a great number of all ages. I have also represented the feet of an individual between two and three years old, on account of the richness of their colour at that age, whereas in the adult males they are quite black." Both top and underside views are given of the feet; Audubon inscribed the sketch at left "foot above" and the one at right "foot beneath."

Havell CCLXXI

PLATE 17

GOSHAWK

(Accipiter gentilis)

COOPER'S HAWK

(Accipiter cooperii)

Audubon assembled this group by cutting out his early pastel drawings of a goshawk (at left) and a Cooper's hawk (at right) and pasting them below a spirited water color of an immature goshawk that he did about 1830. The engraver improvised a landscape background for the birds, bringing them into such incongruous perspective that one early reviewer thought Audubon intended the composition to be a caricature. Above all, the montage illustrates how Audubon's talents developed between 1809, when he drew the Cooper's hawk, and 1830.   Havell CXLI

N.º 28. April 31. 1812   Sylvia   Warble

drawn by J.J. Audubon

PLATE 24

GRAY JAY

(Perisoreus canadensis)

"I have represented a pair of these birds on an oak branch, with its rich autumnal tints," Audubon wrote, "and have attached to it the nest of a hornet, having observed the bird in the State of Maine pursuing that insect." He made this drawing on September 26, 1829. Because of its fondness for meat, this bold jay was known in Maine as the carrion bird; Audubon noted that lumberjacks amused themselves with what they called "transporting the carrion bird." They cut a pole about ten feet long, balanced it on the door sill of a hut, and placed a piece of meat on the end outside the entrance. When a jay alighted on the meat, the lumberjack gave a smart blow to the other end, which drove the bird high into the air. The white oak tree *(Quercus alba)* is probably by George Lehman.

Havell CVII

PLATE 25 *(overleaf)*

BLACK VULTURE

(Coragyps atratus)

Audubon's painting of the black vulture, made in 1829, originally consisted only of the bird on the left and the dismembered head of a Virginia deer. Audubon later added the second vulture by cutting out the head and two feet and pasting them onto the painting. Audubon's first scientific paper, his "maiden speech" as he called it, dealt with the habits of vultures, which he claimed find food by sight, not smell. The paper was read by a friend, with Audubon in attendance, at a meeting of the Wernerian Society of Edinburgh on December 16, 1826. Although Audubon's thesis was much controverted at the time, he was correct.   Havell CVI

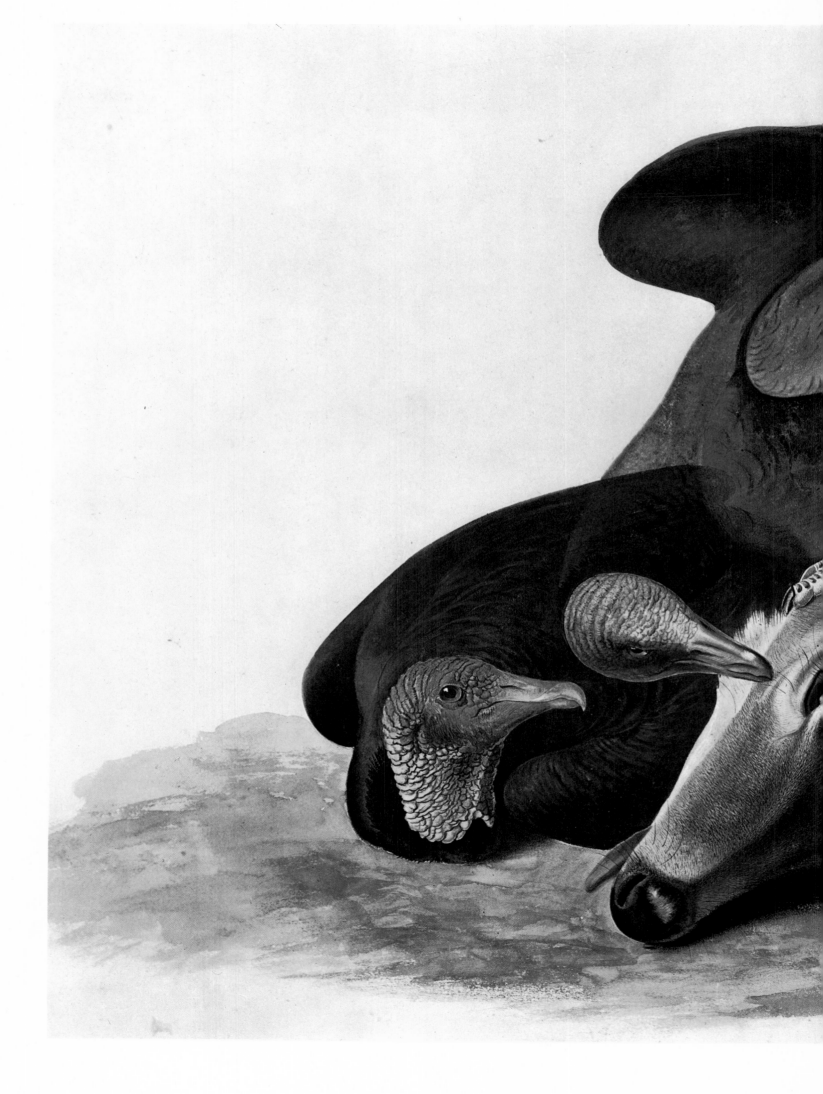

PLATE 26

SCREECH OWL
(Otus asio)

"I carried one of the young birds represented in the plate in my coat pocket," Audubon wrote, "from Philadelphia to New York, travelling alternately by water and by land. It remained generally quiet, fed from the hand, and never attempted to escape." This drawing is inscribed in pencil, "New Jersey Oct^r." The two birds at bottom were rendered in water color in 1829; the bird at top was drawn in pastel (with eyes, bill, and foot in water color) about 1812 and was cut out and pasted onto the later painting. All three are adults: in this species there is often a variation in the color of the plumage, comparable to the different colors of hair and eyes among humans. The owls are perched on the branches of a Jersey, or scrub, pine tree *(Pinus virginiana)*.   Havel XCVII

Mottled Owl Adult 1.
Strix asio
Plant Pinus inops
Vulgo Jersey Pine

Nº 26.
Plate 97.

PLATE 27

BOREAL CHICKADEE

(Parus hudsonicus)

Audubon recorded in his journal that early on the morning of July 18, 1833, he set out from the schooner *Ripley*, anchored off Labrador, to explore the coastal marshes for unknown species. Although he found none that day, he did see a group of these chickadees. This water color was finished two days later, according to the inscription at lower right: "Labrador July 20th 1833 Opposite Island by Macatine." The plant is probably black chokeberry *(Aronia melanocarpa)*.   Havell CXCIV

PLATE 28

TUFTED PUFFIN

(*Lunda cirrhata*)

In his inscription Audubon called this species "Tufted Auk, *Mormon cirrhatus*"; he probably did the painting in Great Britain in 1834 or 1835, using a preserved specimen.   Havell CCXLIX

PLATE 29

SURF SCOTER

(*Melanitta perspicillata*)

Audubon painted this pair of surf scoters (a male at left, a female at right) during his voyage to Labrador in 1833.   Havell CCCXVII

No. 50.   Tufted Auk. adult male.
Mormon cirrhatus, Temm.

Plate 249.

PLATE 30

PIGEON HAWK

(Falco columbarius)

Audubon painted these predators in the East in 1829. A male is shown at top with a female, which is slightly larger, below him. Both appear to be young birds; an adult male of this species is the subject of Plate 156. In his engraving Havell added leaves to the lower portion of the bare branch.

Havell XCII

No 19.
Plate 92.

Pigeon Hawk. Male 1. F. 2.
Falco columbarius.

PLATE 31

HUDSONIAN GODWIT

(Limosa haemastica)

The position in which Audubon drew a bird was often dictated by his wish to show some characteristic marking. In the case of the godwit in breeding plumage, at left, Audubon wanted, as he said, "to shew the difference between this species and the *Limosa melanura* of Europe . . . from which it may readily be distinguished . . . by the black colour of the inner wing-coverts." Audubon probably made this drawing in London in the spring of 1835 from stuffed specimens. His son John drew the godwit at right, in winter plumage, in Boston in 1832.   Havell CCLVIII

PLATE 32

HORNED GREBE

(Podiceps auritus)

Audubon probably painted this species, in spring plumage at left and in winter plumage at right, in Charleston in 1833 or 1834. "Excepting a species of Hawk," he wrote, " . . . I know of no other bird that has the eye of such colour, the iris being externally of a vivid red, with an inner circle of white, which gives it a very singular appearance."   Havell CCLIX

Hudsonian Godwit, Male 1 Young, Female 2, Summer Plumage.
LIMOSA HUDSONICA, Swain, and Richard.

Horned Grebe, adult male, Winter Plumage, Young, Richard.

PLATE 33

SEASIDE SPARROW

(Ammospiza maritima)

Audubon drew these birds, which he called "Sea Side Finches," at Great
Egg Harbor, New Jersey, as inscribed, on June 14, 1829. He observed
them feeding on insects and crustaceans: "Having one day shot a number
of these birds, merely for the sake of practice, I had them made into a pie,
which, however, could not be eaten, on account of its fishy savour." "The
Rose on which I have drawn these birds," he continued, "is found so near
the sea, on rather higher lands than the marshes, that I thought it as fit
as any other plant for the purpose. . . ." The nomenclature of roses is so
intricate that Audubon may be excused for identifying this wild rose as
Rosa carolina; it is actually *Rosa virginiana.* Havell XCIII

Plant. Rosa Carolina
Vulg. Wild Rose.

No 19.
Plate 93.

Sea Side Finch.
Fringilla maritima

PLATE 34

GREAT GRAY OWL

(Strix nebulosa)

Beneath the branch Audubon wrote a note (indistinct on the original, unless examined under special light) to Havell: "Rise the Bird about 4 Inches on the Copper higher than in this Drawing and put a Landscape below of Wild Mountains. . . ." Havell neglected to add a landscape, but he did move the owl up on the page and added several inches to the upper portion of the branch. Audubon probably drew this subject in London between 1834 and 1836. Havell CCCLI

PLATE 35 *(overleaf)*

ROSEATE SPOONBILL

(Ajaia ajaja)

The background for this painting, made in 1831 or 1832 in Florida, was probably penciled in by Lehman and completed by Havell in his engraving. Lehman may well have painted the rest of the habitat and, indeed, the spoonbill itself; Audubon rendered his birds in flatter, less dramatic light. However, the bird's pose and the composition were unquestionably determined by Audubon. "This beautiful and singular bird," Audubon noted, was prized for its wing and tail feathers, which were made into fans—"a regular article of trade" in St. Augustine. Hunters took their toll, and even today the species continues to dwindle. Havell CCCXXI

PLATE 40

FORK-TAILED FLYCATCHER

(Muscivora tyrannus)

"In the end of June 1832," Audubon wrote, "I observed one of these birds a few miles below the city of Camden [New Jersey], flying over a meadow in pursuit of insects, after which it alighted on the top of a small detached tree, where I followed it and succeeded in obtaining it. The bird appeared to have lost itself: it was unsuspicious, and paid no attention to me as I approached it." He used the captured bird to make this drawing. At lower left there is a pencil sketch and notation on the shape of the bird's primary feathers; this, however, was omitted in Havell's engraving. Audubon saw only three other birds of this species: one that was brought to him dead at Henderson, Kentucky, and two that he saw "high in the air" near Natchez, Mississippi. The American Ornithologists' Union *Checklist* records only seven sightings of this bird, a South American species which occasionally is swept northward by tropical hurricanes. In his text, Audubon credits the drawing of the loblolly-bay *(Gordonia lasianthus)* to Maria Martin.   Havell CLXVIII

Lobloly Bay. Gordonia Lasyanthus Mich.

PLATE 41

SANDHILL CRANE

(Grus canadensis)

During his stay in Boston, in the winter of 1832–33, Audubon drew this sandhill crane (believing it to be, and identifying it as, a young whooping crane) from a live specimen. In Havell's engraving ten whooping cranes were added to Audubon's background of Florida sand hills. The pastels Audubon used for the bird's feathers have been partially rubbed off on the right, marring the detail.   Havell CCLXI

PLATE 42

RED-SHOULDERED HAWK

(Buteo lineatus)

Audubon's ability to portray the brutal aspects of nature is demonstrated in this painting of a male hawk seizing a bullfrog. The bird was probably painted in Louisiana about 1822; the frog and the hawk's foot were done separately and pasted onto the drawing. The habitat, filled in some time later, was painted principally in oil. Audubon argued with other naturalists about the bird. He called it a "winter hawk," as inscribed, because he saw it only in winter time. Actually, it is an immature red-shouldered hawk, and Alexander Wilson and Charles Lucien Bonaparte correctly identified it as such.

Havell LXXI

PLATE 43

BONAPARTE'S GULL

(Larus philadelphia)

All three birds in this plate were drawn separately; then Audubon pasted them onto a background and filled in the tail and lower body of the bird at center. The young gull in the foreground probably dates from after 1830; the adult birds were probably painted in Louisiana about 1821. The lower bill of the bird at top has been torn away.   Havell CCCXXIV

PLATE 44

MOCKINGBIRD

(Mimus polyglottos)

Audubon was severely criticized when this dramatic painting was published in 1827. Rattlesnakes neither climb trees, his detractors claimed, nor do they have fangs that curve outward at their tips. Audubon, however, was correct on both points. Other critics objected to the "distorted" positions of his birds, like that of the mockingbird at upper right in this composition. This painting was completed about 1825. (The rattlesnake in striking position was probably copied from a drawing Audubon made at Oakley Plantation in Louisiana, on August 25, 1821.) The vertical portion of the snake's tail was painted after the yellow jessamine vine *(Gelsemium sempervirens)* was completed.

Havell XXI

PLATE 45 *(overleaf)*

SWALLOW-TAILED KITE

(Elanoides forficatus)

"The flight of this elegant species of Hawk is singularly beautiful and protracted. . . . They sweep close over the fields, sometimes seeming to alight for a moment to secure a snake, and holding it fast by the neck, carry it off, and devour it in the air. . . . The common name of the Snake represented in this plate is the Garter Snake." Audubon wrote in his journal that after landing at Bayou Sarah on June 18, 1821, he and Joseph Mason set out on foot for Oakley Plantation, several miles distant. He was delighted by the abundance of wildlife: "My Eyes soon Met hovering over us the Long Wished for, Mississippi Kite and Swallow Tailed Hawk, but our Guns Were pack[d] and We could only then anticipate the pleasure of procuring them shortly." This superb painting was made during that productive summer of 1821. Today this species has disappeared from many parts of the United States.

Havell LXXII

Nº. 15. Plate 72.—
Published 1829.

Swallow-tailed Haw
Falco furcatus
reptile
vulgo— Garter

Fem.^e the Same.—

PLATE 46

CANADA WARBLER
(Wilsonia canadensis)

Inscribed "Great Pine Swamp Augst 1st," this was the first painting Audubon made in the Great Pine Forest in 1829. In his essay on his visit to this once majestic forest in western Pennsylvania, Audubon related that he had just begun exploring the woods when he shot a lovely warbler he had long searched for in vain. He asked a young man with him to break off a twig of great-laurel *(Rhododendron maximum)* and, returning to the house where he was staying, Audubon made this water color of a pair of Canada warblers; another example of this species appears in Plate 6.

Havell CIII

PLATE 49

ROUGH-LEGGED HAWK

(*Buteo lagopus*)

This painting is inscribed, at lower right, "New Jersey July 1832 J J A."
If Audubon did indeed figure this species at that time in New Jersey, he
must have done it from a preserved specimen, since the rough-legged hawk
is not found in that region during July. Later, while Audubon was in
Boston during the winter of 1832, he wrote that he was so anxious to
study these hawks that he offered "premiums for birds . . . and received
as many as eight at one time, of which not one resembled another in the
colour of the plumage, although they were precisely similar in form and
internal structure. The females were similar to the males, but were distinguished by their superior size. . . . I have given you the figure of what
I suppose to have been a middle-aged bird."   Havell CLXVI

PLATE 50

ROBIN

(Turdus migratorius)

Audubon drew the familiar robin three times—first in New York in 1807, next about 1822, and finally at Great Egg Harbor in New Jersey on July 2, 1829. The 1829 painting is reproduced here. "The gentle and lively disposition of the Robin when raised in the cage, and the simplicity of his song, of which he is very lavish in confinement, render him a special favourite," Audubon relates in his text. "It will follow its owner, and come to his call, peck at his finger, or kiss his mouth, with seeming pleasure. It is a long-lived bird, and instances are reported of its having been kept for nearly twenty years." The caterpillar, which an adult is feeding to the young, was finished in Havell's engraving. The branch belongs to what appears to be a chestnut oak *(Quercus prinus)*. Havell CXXXI

PLATE 51

RUDDY TURNSTONE

(Arenaria interpres)

"My drawing of the Turnstones," Audubon wrote, " . . . was made at
Philadelphia, in the end of May 1824; and the beautiful specimen exhibited in the act of flying, I procured near Camden, while in the agree-
able company of my talented friend Le Sueur." (Charles Alexandre
Lesueur, a French artist-naturalist, was among a number of scientists who
in 1825 settled at New Harmony, Robert Owen's Utopian community in
Indiana.) Audubon's painting shows this species both in breeding plumage,
at left, and winter plumage, at right. In any season, the bird's coloration
is so variegated that it is often called the calico bird.   Havell CCCIV

PLATE 52

AMERICAN GOLDEN PLOVER

(Pluvialis dominica)

On March 16, 1821, near New Orleans, Audubon witnessed the passage of
thousands of these birds, coming from the northeast. He had joined a
group of French hunters who, according to his calculations, shot 48,000
plovers in the course of the day. The pastel drawing of the bird on the
left, which is molting, apparently dates from about 1815. It was cut out
and pasted onto the paper, as was the bird in flight. The two plovers on
the right, in breeding plumage, may have been drawn in the 1830's. In
pencil, which has been partially erased, Audubon instructed Havell to
move the bird in flight forward and to turn the bird on the left to face in
the opposite direction (faint outlines indicate the desired position of the
feet). Havell made these changes and added a landscape.   Havell CCC

PLATE 53

MAGPIE-JAY
(Calocitta formosa)

"The specimen from which the drawings were taken," Audubon wrote of
this subject (published in 1830), "was presented to me by a friend who had
received it from the Columbia River, and is the only individual . . . which
I did not myself procure on the spot." Audubon had resolved from the first
never to draw from a stuffed specimen; this marks the first instance in
which he departed from his resolution—and, as a result of his departure,
he erred. He assigned the bird to the region of the Columbia River in
Oregon. It is, in fact, a native of Mexico. Each jay was painted separately
and pasted onto the composition in 1829; they are perched on a dead limb
entwined with poison ivy *(Rhus radicans)*.   Havell XCVI

Pinus pendula
vulgo Black Larch

PLATE 58

WATER PIPIT

(Anthus spinoletta)

Audubon correctly recognized this bird as being identical to the water pipits he had seen in Europe. This drawing was not inscribed, nor was it dated in any of Audubon's writings. It appears to be an early work, possibly done in Kentucky before 1819, and it was among the more than two hundred drawings he exhibited in Edinburgh in 1826. The male water pipit (at left) and his mate are shown in pursuit of an insect, possibly a later addition to the drawing.   Havell X

PLATE 59

BROWN-HEADED COWBIRD

(Molothrus ater)

Audubon apparently drew this pair of cowbirds (the male is at right) in 1824. In a letter written in Philadelphia, on July 14 of that year, he thanked his friend Edward Harris for sending him two cowbirds of which he said he had just made a painting. "If we are fond of admiring the wisdom of Nature," Audubon wrote in his text, "we ought to mingle reason with our admiration. . . . " This bird lays its egg in the nest of another species, and—"remarkable occurrence"—the young cowbird invariably hatches first. The "foster parents" by instinct care for it, thus neglecting their own unhatched eggs, "and the chicks which they contain necessarily perish." Speculating on the justice of this situation, Audubon concluded, "This is a mystery to me; nevertheless, my belief in the wisdom of Nature is not staggered by it."   Havell XCIX

Cow Bunting male & fe.
Icterus pecoris

PLATE 60

SNOWY OWL

(Nyctea scandiaca)

This handsome painting was probably done in 1829 on the east coast; it is the only night scene painted by Audubon for *The Birds of America*. He used pencil to imitate the owl's soft, downy feathers. In his text he tells how this bird caught fish by lying down on its side near the water: "One might have supposed the bird sound asleep, as it would remain in the same position until a good opportunity of securing a fish occurred . . . as the latter unwittingly rose to the surface, near the edge, that instant the Owl thrust out the foot next the water, and, with the quickness of lightning, seized it, and drew it out." The male owl is shown at top, the female is below him.

Havell CXXI

PLATE 61

SOOTY TERN

(Sterna fuscata)

Audubon painted this water color of an adult in breeding plumage on May 10, 1832, in the Dry Tortugas, a small group of islands to the west of the Florida Keys.   Havell CCXXXV

PLATE 62

FULMAR

(Fulmarus glacialis)

Audubon made a pencil sketch of a fulmar off the coast of Newfoundland in late August of 1831. The painting itself was probably not completed until several years later.   Havell CCLXIV

Fulmar Petrel
PROCELLARIA GLACIALIS, L. Male, adult; Summer plumage.

Cinereous Petril, male
Puffinus cinereus, Cuv.

Nº 57. Plate 283.

PLATE 70

BLUE JAY

(Cyanocitta cristata)

"Reader, look at the plate in which are represented three individuals of this beautiful species,—rogues though they be, and thieves, as I would call them, were it fit for me to pass judgment on their actions. See how each is enjoying the fruits of his knavery, sucking the egg which he has pilfered from the nest of some innocent dove or harmless partridge! Who could imagine that a form so graceful, arrayed by nature in a garb so resplendent, should harbour so much mischief;—that selfishness, duplicity, and malice should form the moral accompaniments of so much physical perfection! Yet so it is, and how like beings of a much higher order, are these gay deceivers! Aye, I could write you a whole chapter on this subject, were not my task of a different nature." The painting about which Audubon philosophized was done about 1825. The plant is unfinished: Audubon outlined it in pencil, indicated the leaves with India ink, and instructed Havell to copy the rest from the cross-vine, or trumpet-flower, in Plate 385. Havell CII

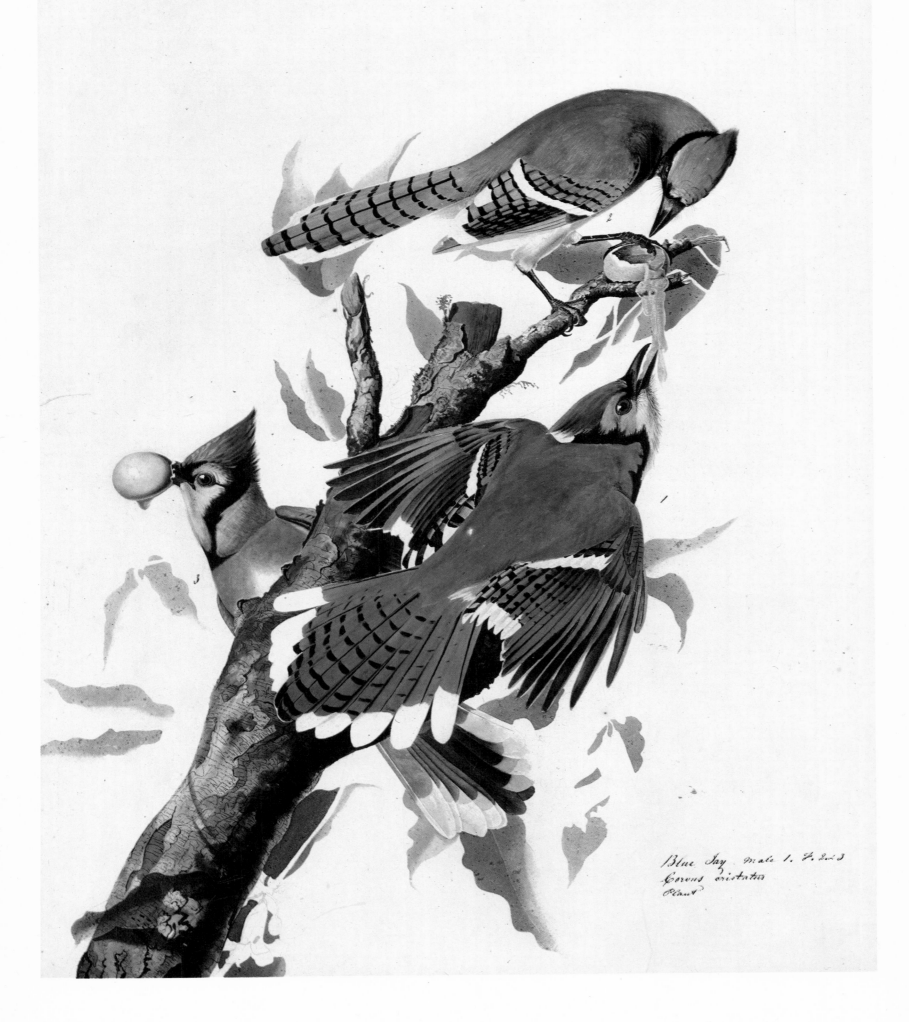

Blue Jay. Male 1. F. 2 & 3
Corvus cristatus
Plant

PLATE 71

RINGED PLOVER
(Charadrius hiaticula)

Audubon used pencil, water color, and pastel on this drawing, which he inscribed "Philadelphia. May 11th 1824." The male plover, at left, is intent upon a snail. The bird at right is a female, probably drawn about 1832. Both plovers are in breeding plumage.   Havell CCCXXX

PLATE 72

WHITE-RUMPED SANDPIPER
(Erolia fuscicollis)

"My drawing of the two individuals represented in the plate," Audubon wrote, "was made at St. Augustine in East Florida, where I procured them on the 2d December 1831." The strikingly detailed background was painted by George Lehman.   Havell CCLXXVIII

PLATE 73

CHESTNUT-BACKED CHICKADEE
(Parus rufescens)

COMMON BUSHTIT
(Psaltriparus minimus)

BLACK-CAPPED CHICKADEE
(Parus atricapillus)

The chestnut-backed chickadees, on the left, and the common bushtits, at right, are western birds, which were collected by Dr. John Kirk Townsend, an ornithologist. Audubon combined them with a pair of eastern birds, the black-capped chickadees, in this painting, which he made in Charleston during the winter of 1836. The nest, belonging to the bushtits, and the branches of the willow oak *(Quercus phellos)* were done by Maria Martin.

Havell CCCLIII

Chesnut-backed Titmouse. 1. male. 2. Female
Parus rufescens. Townsend.

Black-capt Titmouse 3. male 4 ♀.
Parus atricapillus, Wils.
Willow Oak. Quercus phillos L.

Chesnut crowned Titmouse. 5. m. 6.
Parus minimus, Townsend. —
and nest.

Nº 71.

Plate 353—

PLATE 74

AMERICAN FLAMINGO

(Phoenicopterus ruber)

Audubon saw several flocks of American flamingos in the Florida Keys in 1832, and he was exceedingly anxious to obtain a specimen from which he could make a painting. While in London, he wrote repeatedly to his friend Bachman in Charleston asking for one. On August 14, 1837, he wrote: "P.S. Pray send us whatever Captain Coste may have collected for me round the Floridas; and I hope that you will also have some flamingos from Matenzas for me—." Then, on October 31, he wrote again: "As to flamingos their Eggs &c I fear this is up for me; and this proves to me now that I was a great fool not to have gone to Cuba, or sent a person there expressly.—" On December 28 of that year, he insisted once more, "When will the flamingos come???" He finally obtained specimens from Cuba and made this drawing in London in 1838. The somewhat spotted appearance of the flamingo's feathers is caused by the drying of the egg white that was applied over the water color.   Havell CCCCXXXI

PLATE 75 *(overleaf)*

KING EIDER

(Somateria spectabilis)

Audubon has provided these birds (a male at left, a female at right) with a habitat resembling the rocky North Atlantic coast. The drawing may have been done in Boston during the winter of 1832–33.   Havell CCLXXVI

No. 56. Plate 276.

King
Fuligul

2

PLATE 76

RED-TAILED HAWK
(Buteo jamaicensis)

Audubon states that after raising their young, these birds often become hostile toward their mates, robbing each other of their prey. "It was after witnessing such an encounter between two of these powerful marauders, fighting hard for a young Hare, that I made the drawing, in which you perceive the male to have greatly the advantage over the female, although she still holds the prey firmly in one of her talons, even while she is driven towards the earth, with her breast upwards." This dramatic painting was done in Louisiana in 1821 and reworked later. The rabbit's fur is drawn principally in ink.   Havell LI

PLATE 82

LESSER YELLOWLEGS

(Totanus flavipes)

George Lehman quite possibly painted this entire composition—bird and habitat—near Charleston, while he was working in the South with Audubon in 1832. The South Carolina landscape is one of the finest that he painted for *The Birds of America*.   Havell CCLXXXVIII

PLATE 83

YELLOW-THROATED VIREO

(*Vireo flavifrons*)

According to the inscription, Audubon made this drawing at James Pirrie's plantation in Louisiana on July 11, 1821. The vireo, perched on a branch of what Audubon identified as "Swamp Snow-ball," reaches for a wasp. The plant *(Hydrangea quercifolia)* is by Joseph Mason.   Havell CXIX

No. 10.
Plate 49.
(119)

Yellow Throated Vireo. ———— Male.
Vireo flavifrons. +
Plant vulgo Swamp Snow-ball.
Hydrangea quercifolia

Drawn from Nature by John J. Audubon
Louis. Parina; Plantation Louisiana July 11th 1825.

PLATE 84

OSPREY

(Pandion haliaetus)

This painting was undoubtedly done during Audubon's visit to Great Egg Harbor, New Jersey, in June, 1829. A faint notation, visible only upon close examination of the original, reads: "begun Friday at 11 O'clock finished Sunday evening." Audubon wrote in his text, "The largest fish which I have seen this bird take out of the water, was a Weak-Fish, such as is represented in the plate, but sufficiently large to weigh more than five pounds. The bird carried it into the air with difficulty, and dropped it, on hearing the report of a gun fired at it."

Havell LXXXI

PLATE 85 *(overleaf)*

WHITE-FRONTED GOOSE

(Anser albifrons)

Judging from Audubon's text, and his journals, he apparently recorded this species several times. He mentions having shown a drawing of the bird to Alexander Wilson, probably in 1810. In his journal he wrote on November 13, 1821, that he had drawn the species; and a rendering of the white-fronted goose was exhibited in Edinburgh in 1826. Audubon painted this version probably in 1832 or 1833 on the northern Atlantic coast, and it was the basis for Havell's engraving.   Havell CCLXXXVI

N°17. Plate 81

Fish Hawk. *Male*
Falco haliætus
Fish. Vulg. Weak-Fish

n. 58.   White
ANS

Goose, *Lath.*

, Bechst.

. 2.

Plate 286.

PLATE 86

PURPLE MARTIN
(Progne subis)

Audubon observed that Indians frequently hollowed out gourds and hung them near their camps; the gourds were then taken over by martins, which were so audacious that they chased away the vultures attracted to the Indians' venison. "Almost every country tavern has a Martin box on the upper part of its sign-board," Audubon noted, "and I have observed that the handsomer the box, the better does the inn generally prove to be." This painting was done in Mississippi or Louisiana in 1822. The two birds at left are males, and the two at right are females; they are gathered about a gourd *(Lagenaria siceraria)* like the ones that Audubon described.

Havell XXII

PLATE 89

HENSLOW'S SPARROW
(Passerherbulus henslowii)

In 1820, in a field across the Ohio River from Cincinnati, Audubon shot a small bird on the ground amid tall grass. He was the first to describe the bird; he named it in honor of John S. Henslow, professor of botany at the University of Cambridge, whom Audubon met in England during the time Charles Darwin was Henslow's pupil. The discovery of this drab little sparrow, easily overlooked, is testament to Audubon's remarkable abilities as a field naturalist. The painting is signed and dated April 12, 1820; a sketch at lower left shows (as Audubon has written underneath) the "shape of tail" as seen from above the bird. The plants illustrated here also appear in his drawing of the Savannah sparrow (see Plate 246); the worm-grass *(Spigelia marilandica)* is correctly identified, but the other flower (2) is *Verbena canadensis*.   Havell LXX

Henslow's Bunting
Ammodramus Henslowii—
1 Spigelia marilandica
2 Phlox aristata

N°. 14. Plate 70
Published
-1829.-

Drawn at Cincinnati April 12th 1827
by John J. Audubon

PLATE 90

KENTUCKY WARBLER
(Oporornis formosus)

This painting, with habitat by Joseph Mason, was probably done in 1822, when Mason and Audubon were working together in Louisiana and Mississippi. The female bird (at right) was probably painted after the male and flowers were completed; Audubon was often forced to wait until he secured the necessary specimen before he could add a "mate" to his painting of a male or female. Audubon noted that he found this auricled umbrella-tree *(Magnolia fraseri)* only in Mississippi and Louisiana in the grounds preferred by the Kentucky warbler.   Havell XXXVIII

N.º 8. Plate 38. *Kentucky Warbler* Male 1. F. 2.
Sylvia formosa. auriculata
Plant. *Magnolia auriculata*

PLATE 98

YELLOW RAIL

(Coturnicops noveboracensis)

Audubon at first painted this bird surrounded by reeds, which still show
dimly through the landscape painted over the original work. The small
drawing of a feather, at left, appeared in Havell's engraving at upper
right. Audubon made several notations on this drawing; one reported the
results of dissecting the specimen: "Gizzard Large muscular, filled with
shellfish minute & Gravel.—Bird very fat.—Eggs pure white, ready to
Lay on Decr 21. near New Orleans! 1821." Evidently Audubon could not
decide what name to give this bird; he referred to it variously as a "streaked
rail," a "yellow-breasted rail," and, in the inscription on this drawing, a
"New York rail."

Havell CCCXXIX

PLATE 99

RED PHALAROPE

(Phalaropus fulicarius)

Audubon encountered this bird only twice — in Louisville, Kentucky, in
late October, 1808, and years later, in September, 1831, aboard ship about
sixty miles off Nantucket Island. "I have not seen the Red Phalarope alive
on any other occasion," he wrote. This drawing was made in London in
1835 from specimens he received from Captain James Clark Ross, a nephew
of the celebrated explorer Sir John Ross. In most species of birds the male
is brightly colored and takes the active role in courtship. Of phalaropes,
not only is the converse true, but the male is literally henpecked: his
glamourous mate abandons the nest as soon as the eggs are laid, leaving
him behind to hatch and raise the young. Never having observed these
peculiar breeding habits, it is not surprising that Audubon mistakenly
identified the dull gray bird at center as a female; actually it is a male,
flanked by colorful female phalaropes.

Havell CCLV

New York Rail.
Rallus (Crex) noveboracensis.

Plate 255.

No 51 pl 255

Red Phalarope *Adult Male 1. Adult Female 2. Winter Plumage 3.*
Phalaropus platyrhynchus, Temm.

PLATE 100

EASTERN KINGBIRD
(*Tyrannus tyrannus*)

Audubon noted in his text that man persecutes this species "without mercy, and extends his enmity to its whole progeny. This mortal hatred is occasioned by a propensity which the Tyrant Fly-catcher [or kingbird] now and then shows to eat a honey-bee, which the narrow-minded farmer looks upon as exclusively his own property, although he is presently to destroy thousands of its race, for the selfish purpose of seizing upon the fruits of their labours, which he does with as little remorse as if nature's bounties were destined for man alone." In truth, Audubon reported, "the vast number of insects which he devours, and which would otherwise torment the cattle and horses, are benefits conferred by him. . . . " Audubon showed one of this pair of kingbirds eating a honey-bee. The painting is dated April 10, 1822, at which time Audubon and Mason, who painted the cottonwood tree (*Populus deltoides*), were living in Natchez, Mississippi.

Havell LXXIX

Tyrant Flycatcher Male 1. F. 2
Muscicapa tyrannus. —
Plant
Vulgo Cotton wood — Populus candicans

PLATE 101

BLACK-NECKED STILT

(Himantopus mexicanus)

This drawing was done, as inscribed at lower left, in New Orleans, on May 2, 1821. In his journal on that day Audubon wrote, "drew a Long Legged Plover . . . it was a Male I received it from M^r [Ambrose] Duval the Miniature Painter who assured Me that he had Killed 6 or 7 he leaves here, all alike no diference whatever in the size or Coloring . . . Was pleased with the Position in my drawing—." In the engraving, the habitat was greatly simplified, and the boats were deleted.   Havell CCCXXVIII

PLATE 102

HARRIS' HAWK

(Parabuteo unicinctus)

Faintly inscribed, at lower right, "J.J.A 1837," this painting was apparently made in October of that year in London. Audubon named the bird for Edward Harris, who had befriended the artist in Philadelphia in 1824 and had helped him by purchasing some of his early drawings. Audubon wrote to Bachman in 1837, "Harris . . . is in fact one of the finest Men of God's creation—I wish he was my Brother."   Havell CCCXCII

Drawn from Nature by John J. Audubon
New Orleans May 2d 1831

Long legged Plover   Male
Charadrius Himantopus

PLATE 103

BAY-BREASTED WARBLER

(Dendroica castanea)

The inscription—"Drawn May 12th 1812. Pens[a]"—no doubt refers to an early sketch from which Audubon copied this painting in about 1825. This pair of warblers, with the male at left, was painted in water color; pastel was added, over the water color, on the breasts. The upland cotton plant *(Gossypium herbaceum)*, as well as the birds, appears to be the work of Audubon.   Havell LXIX

Bay breasted Warbler. *Male 1 & Fem. 2.*
Sylvia castanea
Plant Tulip. Highland Cotton
Gossipium herbaceum.

N° 14. Plate 69.

Ed. Ling.
1829. —

Drawn May 15th 1812 Sent to
R. of S. N.

PLATE 104

COMMON GRACKLE

(*Quiscalus quiscula*)

Audubon was obviously proud of the striking characterization he achieved in this painting, which was probably made in Louisiana about 1825. "Look at them," he wrote. "The male, as if full of delight at the sight of the havoc which he has already committed on the tender, juicy, unripe corn on which he stands, has swelled his throat, and is calling in exultation to his companions to come and assist him in demolishing it. The female has fed herself, and is about to fly off with a well-loaded bill to her hungry and expectant brood. . . . See how the husk is torn from the ear, and how nearly devoured are the grains of corn [*Zea mays*]!"   Havell VII

PLATE 105 *(overleaf)*

BARNACLE GOOSE

(*Branta leucopsis*)

Audubon had never seen any live specimens of these geese. "Being neither anxious to add to our Fauna," he wrote in his text, "nor willing unnecessarily to detract from it, I have figured a pair of these birds, with the hope that ere long, the assertions of [others] . . . may be abundantly verified by the slaughter of many geese." Actually the barnacle goose is an Old World species, and Audubon would have been wise to omit it from his publication. Although a few breed in Greenland, this goose almost never visits the North American continent. Audubon apparently drew the bird from mounted specimens in Great Britain between 1834 and 1836. The rendering of the habitat, done with oil paints, suggests the work of his son Victor.   Havell CCXCVI

PLATE 106

BALD EAGLE

(Haliaeetus leucocephalus)

Audubon probably painted this young eagle in the East during the summer of 1829. The bald eagle does not acquire its distinctive white head and tail, nor its yellow iris and beak, until it is three or four years old. A somewhat older bird of this species is shown in Plate 228, and the splendid, full-fledged adult appears in Plate 2.   Havell CXXVI

PLATE 107

PINE GROSBEAK
(Pinicola enucleator)

Audubon's younger son, John, may have assisted on this drawing, which was probably done during the winter of 1833–34 in Charleston. The red bird at bottom is an adult male; above him is an adult female; and the topmost bird is an immature grosbeak. In his text, Audubon wrote that his son brought back a number of these birds from Newfoundland. "It was curious to see how covered with sores the legs of the old birds of both sexes were. These sores or excrescences are, I believe, produced by the resinous matter of the fir-trees on which they obtain their food . . . and I was surprised that the birds had not found means of ridding themselves of such an inconvenience." The male bird is shown with these sores, and beneath the bird Audubon instructed the engraver, "pay attention to make diseased legs!" The branch appears to be that of a scrub pine *(Pinus virginiana)* or a shortleaf pine *(Pinus echinata)*.   Havell CCCLVIII

PINE GROSBEAK.

Nº 72.   Pyrrhula enucleator

Pl. 358

PLATE 108

GLOSSY IBIS
(Plegadis falcinellus)

"The Glossy Ibis," Audubon wrote, "is of exceedingly rare occurrence in the United States, where it appears only at long and irregular intervals, like a wanderer who has lost his way. . . . I have given the figure of a male bird in superb plumage, procured in Florida. . . . " Audubon wrote his wife from St. Augustine, on January 16, 1832, saying that he had collected a new ibis, possibly a member of this species. The drawing itself could not have been done before 1836, the watermark date on the paper; possibly it was done in the winter of 1836–37 in Charleston.   Havell CCCLXXXVII

PLATE 109

BARROW'S GOLDENEYE
(Bucephala islandica)

Audubon appears to have drawn this male goldeneye in 1838 in London. The specimen was given to the artist by the Earl of Derby, who in turn obtained it from a member of an Arctic expedition. Havell added water and sky to his engraving of this work.   Havell CCCCIII

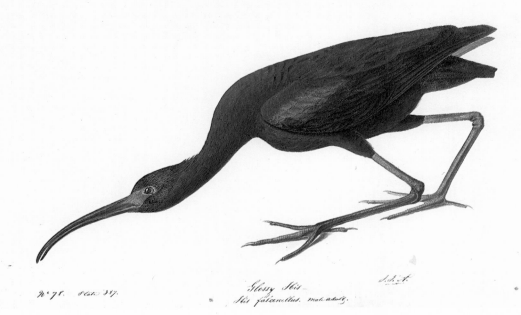

No. 78.   Plate 387.   Glossy Ibis   J.J.A.
                         Ibis falcinellus. Male adult.

No. 387   Plate 388.

        Golden eyed Duck   Summer Plumage? Male.
              Clangula vulgaris.

PLATE 110

BARN OWL

(Tyto alba)

This pair of owls was given to Audubon, as he wrote in his text, "by my friend Richard Harlan, M.D., of Philadelphia. They had been brought from the south, and were fine adult birds in excellent plumage. I have placed a ground squirrel under the feet of one of them, as being an animal on which the species is likely to feed." In Havell's engraving of this plate a night scene was added as background. The drawing is inscribed at lower left "New Jersey July 1832."   Havell CLXXI

Winged B. W. (...)
Length from bill to base of (...)
Tail (...)
Breadth (...)
3 feet (...)
3 of 8 Primaries (...)
New Orleans Feby. 1822
J. J. A.

PLATE 111

CRESTED BOBWHITE
(*Colinus cristatus*)

MOUNTAIN QUAIL
(*Oreortyx pictus*)

Audubon probably made this composition in London in 1838. The crested bobwhite, at right, was drawn from a specimen in the collection of the Museum of the Zoological Society of London; it is a tropical bird, included erroneously in *The Birds of America*. The male mountain quail, at left, was drawn from a specimen in the same collection, and its mate, at center, was done from a specimen collected by Dr. Townsend. In Havell's engraving, a landscape was added as background, and the bobwhite, a cut-out, was turned around to face the mountain quail.   Havell CCCCXXIII

PLATE 112

CRESTED AUKLET
(*Aethia cristatella*)

ANCIENT MURRELET
(*Synthliboramphus antiquum*)

LEAST AUKLET
(*Aethia pusilla*)

RHINOCEROS AUKLET
(*Cerorhinca monocerata*)

All of these birds (identified, from left to right, as listed above) were drawn from specimens, probably in London in 1837. Both an adult (1) and a young (2) murrelet are shown. In Havell's engraving an icy landscape was added to suggest America's northwestern coast.   Havell CCCCII

Phaleris superciliata, Bonap.
Curled-crested Auk.

Mergulus antiquus, Bonap.
1 Adult 2 Young
Black-throated Guillemot.

Phaleris nodirostris, Bonap.
Knobbed-billed Auk.

Ceratorhina Occidentalis, Bonap.
Horned-billed Guillemot.

PLATE 113

CAROLINA WREN

(Thryothorus ludovicianus)

This painting was done in Louisiana or Mississippi in 1822. In terms of its composition and execution it is one of Audubon's and Mason's finest works. Mason painted the blossoming twig, which Audubon identified as a "Dwarf horse chesnut" in his inscription; today it is commonly called scarlet buckeye *(Aesculus pavia)*. Havell LXXVIII

No 16. Plate 78

J. J. Audubon

Great Carolina Wren. Male 1. & 2.
Troglodytes ludovicianus
Plant Vulgo. Dwarf horse chestnut.
Æsculus Pavia

PLATE 114

EASTERN MEADOWLARK
(*Sturnella magna*)

The meadowlark, one of the first birds to arrive in the northern states in spring, moved Audubon to one of the most romantic commentaries in his text. "How could I give the history of this beautiful bird," he wrote, "were I not to return for a while to the spot where I have found it most abundant, and where the most frequent opportunities occurred of observing it? Then, reader, to those rich grass fields let us stray. We are not far from the sandy sea-shores of the Jerseys; the full beauties of an early spring are profusely spread around us; the glorious sun illumines the creation with a flood of golden light. . . ." Audubon's painting portrays one bird in flight, to show its six white tail feathers. The bird in the right foreground, painted before Audubon made this composition in 1829, was cut out and pasted onto the later work. (The species is not in truth a lark; it is rather a member of the family that includes American orioles and blackbirds.) The elaborate background of downy false foxglove (*Aureolaria virginica*) was painted by Lehman. Havell CXXXVI

PLATE 115 *(overleaf)*

LOUISIANA HERON
(*Hydranassa tricolor*)

Despite its name, the Louisiana heron ranges over a wide area, sometimes traveling as far north as New York and west to California. It is most abundant, however, in the coastal areas of the South, and Audubon observed great colonies nesting in the Florida Keys during his trip to that area in the spring of 1832. "Delicate in form, beautiful in plumage, and graceful in its movements," Audubon exclaimed. "Watch its motions, as it leisurely walks over the pure sand beaches of the coast of Florida, arrayed in the full beauty of its spring plumage. Its pendent crest exhibits its glossy tints, its train falls gracefully. . . ." Audubon drew this heron in the spring of 1832; the background, by Lehman, shows a Florida key, or reeflike island, overgrown with low, dense shrubs and graceful royal palms (*Roystonea elata*). Havell CCXVII

PLATE 116

CANADA GOOSE

(Branta canadensis)

Audubon called this bird "Hutchins's barnacle goose"; actually it is a sub-species of the Canada goose (see Plate 94). Audubon heard reports of "this alleged species" in Maine and searched for it there without success. Later he received a specimen from his friend Captain Ross and made this drawing, probably in Great Britain in 1834 or 1835. In Havell's engraving, a land-scape of the Far North appears in the background.   Havell CCLXXVII

Hutchins's barnacle Goose.—
Anser Hutchinsii. Richard.

PLATE 126

BOREAL OWL

(Aegolius funereus)

"I procured a fine male of this species at Bangor, in Maine, on the Penobscot River, in the beginning of September 1832," Audubon wrote, "but am unacquainted with its habits, never having seen another individual alive." In this painting, the specimen is shown both from the side and from the rear. Havell CCCLXXX

PLATE 155

CLIFF SWALLOW
(*Petrochelidon pyrrhonota*)

Audubon first saw this species in 1815 in Kentucky and named it "the *Republican Swallow*, in allusion to the mode in which the individuals belonging to it associate, for the purpose of forming their nests and rearing their young." He lost the specimens taken then and was not able to record his find until years later, in Cincinnati, where he was employed by the Western Museum. Its curator, Robert Best, reported to him the appearance of a "strange species" in the neighborhood of the Ohio River. Audubon rushed to the spot, where "the chirruping of my long-lost little strangers saluted my ear." For several months he observed the swallows building their curious nests, laying eggs, and hatching the young; he did this painting on May 20, 1820; later—possibly in 1825—the rock was drawn on a separate piece of paper that had been pasted beneath the rendering of the nests.   Havell LXVIII

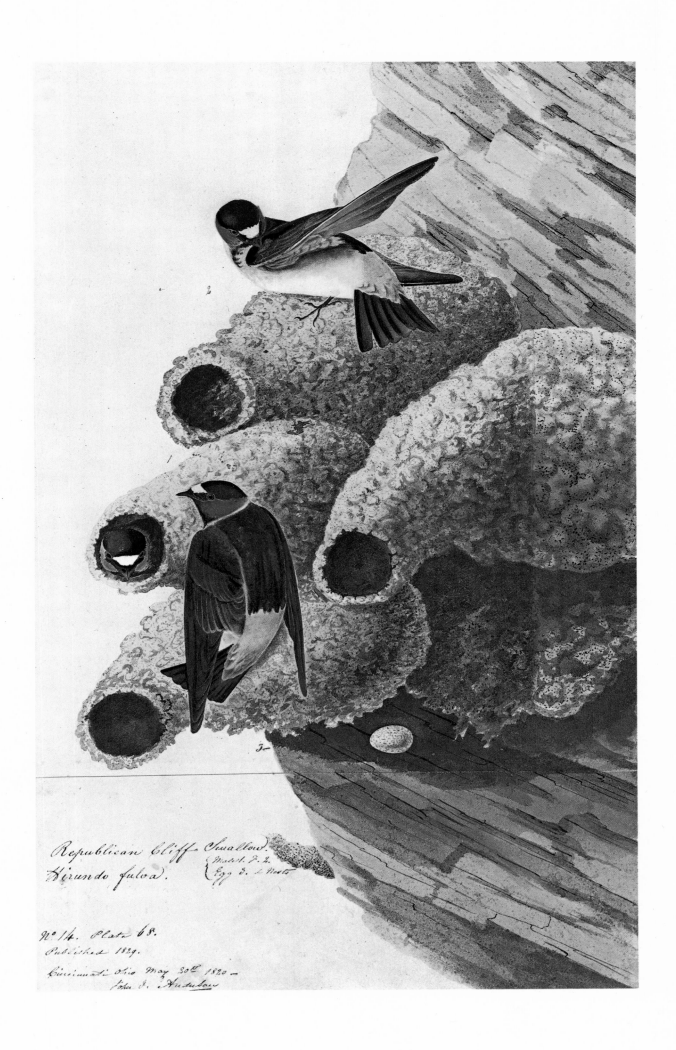

Republican Cliff Swallow.
Hirundo fulva.

No 14. Plate 68.
Published 1829.
Cincinnati Ohio May 20th 1820 —
John J. Audubon

PLATE 134

CLAPPER RAIL
(*Rallus longirostris*)

Audubon drew these birds in Charleston during the winter of 1833–34; the clapper rail on the left was done separately and then pasted beside the other bird. The composition covers an unfinished drawing: the head of another bird is faintly visible through the marsh grasses beneath the clapper rail at left.

Havell CCIV

PLATE 135 *(overleaf)*

KEY WEST QUAIL-DOVE
(*Geotrygon chrysia*)

On May 6, 1832, an American soldier who was acting as Audubon's guide in the Key West region shot one of these beautiful birds. Audubon had never seen this species alive, and he exclaimed: "How I gazed on its resplendent plumage! . . . I handled it, turned it, examined its feathers and form . . . its legs and claws, weighed it by estimate, and after a while formed a winding sheet for it of a piece of paper. Did ever an Egyptian pharmacopolist employ more care in embalming the most illustrious of the Pharaohs, than I did in trying to preserve from injury this most beautiful of the woodland cooers!" "But who will draw it?" he asked himself, recalling a French quotation: "*La nature se joue du pinceau des hommes;— lorsqu'on croit qu'il a atteint sa plus grande beauté, elle sourit et s'embellit encore!*" ("Nature toys with man's paintbrush; just when he thinks he has captured her greatest beauty, she smiles and becomes more lovely than ever!") Nonetheless, Audubon painted this pair—the male is on the left—against a habitat done by Lehman. A clump of leaves is pasted onto the foreground; the large purple flowers belong to the railroad-vine (*Ipomoea pes-caprae*) and the white flowers are those of the rubber-vine (*Echites umbellata*).

Havell CLXVII

PLATE 139

SURFBIRD
(*Aphriza virgata*)

Audubon was never able to realize his ambition of traveling beyond the Rocky Mountains to draw from life the birds native to that region of North America. He had to content himself with working from skins, many of them obtained from Thomas Nuttall and John Kirk Townsend, who in 1834 made an expedition to the mouth of the Columbia River. Townsend sent Audubon a note along with this specimen: "I shot this bird, the only one I have ever seen, on Cape Disappointment, at the entrance of the Columbia River. It was sitting on the edge of the steep rocks, and the heavy surf frequently dashed its spray over it as it foraged among the retreating waves." Audubon probably made this composition in London in 1838. In order to show all the surfbird's markings he made two drawings—a view from below and a view from above—and then pasted the two renderings together.   Havell CCCCXXVIII

PLATE 140

GROUND DOVE

(Columbigallina passerina)

Audubon found this dove in the coastal areas of almost all the southern states, and in Charleston he saw a pair so tame that they mated and reared their young in captivity. A trio of males appears at the top of this composition and below them are a female and a young dove. In a letter to his wife written from Charleston on October 30, 1831, Audubon mentioned that Lehman was at work painting this wild orange branch *(Citrus aurantium)*.

Havell CLXXXII

PLATE 141

HORNED LARK
(*Eremophila alpestris*)

Audubon wrote that he saw many of these birds breeding "on the high and desolate tracts of Labrador, in the vicinity of the sea. The face of the country appears as if formed of one undulated expanse of dark granite, covered with mosses and lichens, varying in size and colour . . . and disposed in large patches or tufts. It is on the latter that the Lark places her nest. . . ." In his journal for July 28, 1833, Audubon also wrote that he had captured three young chicks; the next day he drew them. On the following day he shot and drew a "beautiful male in full summer dress" (seated near the nest). To these he added two more larks, in summer plumage (center) and in winter plumage (right), cut out of a drawing that he had made in March of the same year.   Havell CC

PLATE 142

CALIFORNIA QUAIL
(*Lophortyx californicus*)

This drawing was probably made in London in 1837 from specimens sent to Audubon from California by Dr. Townsend. The female (at left) is reaching for a spider. Havell added a mountain landscape to his engraving.
Havell CCCCXIII

PLATE 143

PURPLE FINCH

(Carpodacus purpureus)

Both the style of this painting, done entirely in water color, and the external evidence—the red larch *(Larix laricina)* is native to the northern United States—indicate that Audubon probably painted these finches in 1824, during a trip to the Great Lakes. The two birds at top are males; the bird below is a female.   Havell IV

PLATE 144

BAND-TAILED PIGEON
(Columba fasciata)

This drawing is probably the most interesting to botanists of all Audubon's published works, since the accompanying text in the *Ornithological Biography* contains the first recorded description of the western, or mountain, dogwood. Both the pigeons and the dogwood were collected by Townsend and Nuttall on their 1834 expedition to the Pacific Northwest. Audubon drew the birds, probably during the winter of 1836–37; the "amiable and accomplished" Maria Martin made "the beautiful drawing of this branch." Audubon named the dogwood *Cornus nuttalli* in honor of its discoverer, Thomas Nuttall.   Havell CCCLXVII

PLATE 145 *(overleaf)*

GREAT CORMORANT
(Phalacrocorax carbo)

"Look at the birds before you, and mark the affectionate glance of the mother, as she stands beside her beloved younglings!" wrote Audubon; "I wish you could have witnessed the actions of such groups as I did while in Labrador." Then he proceeded to describe how, at three o'clock on the morning of July 3, 1833, he crawled along a rocky precipice some hundred feet above the St. Lawrence River and surprised a female cormorant and her brood. "I have witnessed their pleasures and their terrors [at his intrusion], and now, crawling backwards, I leave them to resume their ordinary state of peaceful security." Evidently Audubon could not bring himself to kidnap the chicks; but the next day an assistant brought him a nest, and a week later he obtained a female and two young birds and made this painting, finishing it on July 12. The male, at right, was added later, possibly in March, 1834.   Havell CCLXVI

Nº 74.
Plate 367.

J. J. A.

Band-tailed Pigeon. 1 Male, 2 Female.
Columba fasciata, Say.

Nuttall's Cornel
Cornus Nuttallii, Aud.

PLATE 146

ARCTIC TERN
(Sterna paradisaea)

Audubon first saw this species in early June of 1833 in the Magdalen Islands, off the coast of Nova Scotia. He was enchanted by its movements: "Light as a sylph, the Arctic Tern dances through the air above and around you. The graces, one might imagine, had taught it to perform those beautiful gambols which you see it display. . . ." As his ship continued north toward Labrador, Audubon saw many more Arctic terns, and in his journal for June 25 he wrote that he had made this drawing. It was later cut out and pasted against a painting of the sky.   Havell CCL

PLATE 147

YELLOW WARBLER

(Dendroica petechia)

Although Audubon published two drawings of the yellow warbler in its immature state, believing each to be distinct species (see Plates 263 and 383), he correctly identified this adult male, painted in 1822. "I made my drawing . . . near Natchez," he wrote, "and having killed the specimen while it was searching for insects among the flowers of a large climbing plant, I have figured part of the latter also." In fact, Mason drew the wisteria *(Wisteria frutescens* or *Wisteria macrostachya)*.   Havell XCV

No 19.
Plate 95.

Blue–eyed yellow Warbler.
Sylvia Æstiva
Plant. — Wisteria

PLATE 148

STELLER'S EIDER

(Polysticta stelleri)

"This beautiful species, which was discovered by [Georg Wilhelm] Steller on the north-west coast of America, has never been known to visit our Atlantic shores," Audubon wrote in his text. "So very scarce indeed is it, that all my exertions to obtain a specimen have failed." His son John found a specimen (entitled here "Western Duck") in a museum in Norwich, England, and made this painting, probably in 1838. When Havell made his engraving, he added another male duck standing amid reeds at the water's edge.   Havell CCCCXXIX

PLATE 149

LIMPKIN

(Aramus guarauna)

Audubon found the limpkin in the Florida Everglades. "Although of considerable size and weight," he noted, "they are enabled, by the great length and expansion of their toes to walk on the broad leaves of the larger species of Nymphaea found in that country." He made this drawing in Charleston, South Carolina, in the winter of 1836–37; the background, indicated here in a faint pencil outline, was completed in the engraving.
                                                                Havell CCCLXXVII

N° 86.

Western Duck

PLATE 150

SAW-WHET OWL

(Aegolius acadicus)

"The Little Owl is known in Massachusetts by the name of the 'Saw-whet,'
the sound of its love-notes bearing a great resemblance to the noise produced by filing the teeth of a large saw. These notes, when coming, as
they frequently do, from the interior of a deep forest, produce a very
peculiar effect on the traveller, who, not being aware of their real nature,
expects, as he advances on his route, to meet with shelter under a saw-
mill at no great distance." Audubon confessed that he had been deceived
in this manner more than once. In a letter written on March 19, 1833,
from Boston, he told his son Victor that he had recently made this drawing
of two "Little Owls."   Havell CXCIX

PLATE 151

KILLDEER

(Charadrius vociferus)

This bird, Audubon explained, is "so named on account of its note, which may be imitated by the syllables *kildee, kildee*. . . ." While living at Mill Grove, the farm in Pennsylvania that was his first home in America, Audubon rescued a brood of young killdeer. The son of one of his tenants, he said, had a "barbarous practice" of using newly hatched birds to bait his fishhooks. "One morning I met him returning from the shores of the Perkioming Creek. . . . He endeavoured to avoid me, but I made directly up to him, peeped into his hat and saw the birds. On this I begged of him to . . . restore the poor things to their parents, which he reluctantly did. Never had I felt more happy than I did when I saw [them] run off and hide under cover of the stones." This drawing was made between 1821 and 1825 and was among the works Audubon exhibited at the Royal Institution in Edinburgh in 1826.   Havell CCXXV

PLATE 152

HOODED MERGANSER

(Lophodytes cucullatus)

This pastel and water-color drawing (the habitat being done with the use of stipple) was made in New Orleans in 1821. Of the male, at left, Audubon wrote: "Its broad and rounded crest of pure white, with an edging of jetty black, and which it closes or spreads out at pleasure, renders the male of this species conspicuous on the waters to which it resorts. The activity of its motions, the rapidity of its flight, and its other habits, contribute to render it a pleasing object to the student of nature. . . ."   Havell CCXXXII

PLATE 153

SWAINSON'S WARBLER

(Limnothlypis swainsonii)

This "original Audubon" was painted by Audubon's son John, with flowers and butterflies by Maria Martin. The bird was discovered by John Bachman near Charleston, South Carolina, in the spring of 1832. Audubon himself added to this work only marginally; he sketched the details at lower left. The pencil sketches show the bill and toe of a worm-eating warbler above those of Swainson's warbler, for the sake of contrasting the differences in the features. In his text Audubon introduced his remarks on this warbler by taking to task "one of the wise men of a certain city [Philadelphia] in the United States," who had "assured the members of a Natural History Society there, that no more birds would be found in the country than had been described" by Wilson. Audubon added this bird, named for the English naturalist William Swainson, to a lengthy list of newly discovered species, constituting more new birds, Audubon assured his readers, "than the learned academician probably knew of old ones." The branch on which the warbler stands is a flame azalea (*Rhododendron calendulaceum*). Havell CXCVIII

PLATE 154

BLACK-BILLED MAGPIE

(Pica pica)

Audubon recognized this noisy bird as being identical with the magpie common to all parts of Europe. In North America it lives only in the western regions, and Audubon had to use preserved specimens as models for this drawing, done in England in 1835 or 1836.   Havell CCCLVII

PLATE 155 *(overleaf)*

MALLARD

(Anas platyrhynchos)

This large, easily tamed fowl is the forebear of almost every variety of domesticated duck. But, as Audubon observed, "How brisk are all his motions compared with those of his brethren that waddle across your poultry-yard! how much more graceful in form and neat in apparel! The duck at home is the descendant of a race of slaves . . . But the free-born, the untamed duck of the swamps,—see how he springs on wing, and hies away over the woods." Audubon drew these mallards when he was in Louisiana or Mississippi, sometime between 1821 and 1825. The two drakes are easily distinguished by the coloration of their heads, "glittering with emerald-green." The plants in the foreground were drawn separately and pasted onto the composition.   Havell CCXXI

PLATE 156

PIGEON HAWK

(Falco columbarius)

Thinking this a newly discovered bird, Audubon called it *"Le Petit Capo-ral."* In his text he explained: "The name which I have given to this new and rare species was chosen at the time when Napoleon le Grand was in the zenith of his glory. Every body knows that his soldiers frequently designated him by the nickname of *Le Petit Caporal*, which I thought more suitable to our *little* Hawk, than the names Napoleon, or Bonaparte, which I should have adopted, had I been so fortunate as to procure a new Eagle." The male hawk, not a new species, was drawn entirely by Audubon in pencil and pastel on April 23, 1812, in Pennsylvania, as inscribed. The vine (probably *Smilax rotundifolia*), painted later in water color, was probably done by Joseph Mason.   Havell LXXV

Le petit Caporal
Falco temerarius
Male

Nº 75. Plate 75.
April 23. 1812. Pen.

PLATE 157

ZENAIDA DOVE

(Zenaida aurita)

Audubon wrote that he was always especially fond of doves. "My Father often told me, that when yet a child, my first attempt at drawing was from a preserved specimen of a dove, and many times repeated to me that birds of this kind are usually remarkable for the gentleness of their disposition. . . ." Indeed, Audubon reported that a former pirate who frequented "a well known Key, which must here be nameless," was remarkably affected by some doves that he encountered while pursuing his evil ways: "the soft and melancholy cry of the doves awoke in his breast feelings which had long slumbered, [and] melted his heart to repentance. . . . So deeply moved was he by the notes of any bird, and especially by those of a dove . . . he was induced to . . . return to a family deploring his absence. . . . and now he lives in peace in the midst of his friends." The painting was made in the Florida Keys in the spring of 1832. The branch on which one of the doves is perched, painted by George Lehman, is that of a pond-apple, or alligator-apple, tree *(Anona glabra)*.   Havell CLXII

PLATE 158

STORM PETREL

(Hydrobates pelagicus)

"Becalmed on the banks of Newfoundland" in August of 1831, Audubon collected several specimens of this petrel. The water color was probably completed somewhat later in the mid-1830's. This species is European and is found in the United States infrequently.   Havell CCCXL

PLATE 159

STILT SANDPIPER

(Micropalama himantopus)

This painting, probably done along the Atlantic coast about 1833, may be partly the work of Audubon's son John. The landscape, indicated in pencil, was slightly changed in Havell's engraving. Faintly distinguishable at right, an inscription specifies that the bird has twelve tail feathers.
                                                              Havell CCCXLIV

No 68. Plate 340.

Leach Petrel.

No 69 — Plate 344.   Long legged Sandpiper.   Tringa himantopus, Bonap.

PLATE 160

MOURNING DOVE

(Zenaidura macroura)

In this painting Audubon attempted, as he wrote, to give "a faithful representation of two as gentle pairs of Turtles [doves] as ever cooed their loves in the green woods. I have placed them on a branch of Stuartia, which you see ornamented with a profusion of white blossoms, emblematic of purity and chastity." The painting was probably done about 1825 in Louisiana. The pair of birds at bottom was apparently done first; the topmost bird may have been the last addition Audubon made to the painting, since the limb on which it sits is not connected to the branch on which its mate is perched. The silky-camellia, or Virginia-Stewartia *(Stewartia malachodendron)*, is a member of the tea family, as are *Gordonia* (Plate 40) and *Franklinia* (Plate 419). Havell XVII

PLATE 161

SHORT-BILLED DOWITCHER
(Limnodromus griseus)

"This bird exhibits at times a manner of feeding which appeared to me singular," Audubon wrote. "While watching their manner of walking and wading along sand-bars and muddy flats, I saw that . . . when the water reached their bodies, they immersed the head and a portion of the neck, and remained thus sufficiently long to satisfy me that, while in this position, they probed several spots before raising their head to breathe. On such grounds as are yet soft, although not covered with water, they bore holes as deep as the soil will admit. . . ." Audubon drew these dowitchers on the Atlantic coast in 1832 or 1833, showing them in both winter (left) and summer plumage. Instructing Havell to shorten one of the toes of the bird on the right, he penciled in the note, "Join the toe as now marked excluding the black over it—."   Havell CCCXXXV

PLATE 162

MANX SHEARWATER
(Puffinus puffinus)

This European species seldom visits North America. Audubon saw it off the Newfoundland banks during one of his voyages (probably in August, 1831) from England to America. The drawing was apparently begun in pencil then and finished later, possibly in 1835.   Havell CCXCV

Join No. 180 as now marked
...dding the black one ...

Mark Puffin ... ...
...Puffin angorum, Ray.

PLATE 168

LIGHT-MANTLED SOOTY ALBATROSS
(*Phoebetria palpebrata*)

Audubon wrote in his text that Dr. Townsend provided the skin from which this painting was made, and he stated—probably incorrectly—that the specimen was found near the mouth of the Columbia River in Oregon. In fact, this species breeds in New Zealand and ranges throughout the Southern Hemisphere. The painting may have been done in London in 1838; in Havell's engraving, a background of land and water was added. Audubon noted in pencil near the wing, "first quill longest," and beneath the tail, "12 Feathers very broad."

Havell CCCCVII

PLATE 169

GREAT AUK
(*Pinguinus impennis*)

Audubon probably drew this bird between 1834 and 1836, while he was in London. He never saw a live auk and possessed only one "authentic account of the occurrence of this bird on our coast," from Henry Havell, the brother of Audubon's engraver. One leg of the bird at left was only outlined in pencil; Havell finished the drawing and added a rocky, windswept landscape to his engraving. The great auk was extinct by 1844, as a result of relentless persecution by sealers.

Havell CCCXLI

Brown Albatros
Diomedea fulva.

N° 82. Plate 407.

PLATE 170

LEAST TERN
(Sterna albifrons)

The young tern above and the adult below were drawn separately and
pasted onto the background of the sky. The adult was drawn in Louisiana
in 1821; the young bird may have been done in 1833. "Nothing can
exceed the lightness of the flight of this bird," Audubon wrote of the least
tern, "which seems to me to be among water-fowls, the analogue of the
Humming-bird. They move with great swiftness at times, at others balance
themselves like hawks . . . then dart with the velocity of thought to procure the tiny fry beneath the surface. . . ."   Havell CCCXIX

Lesser Tern. Adult 1. Young 2

STERNA MINUTA, L.

PLATE 177

RUSTY BLACKBIRD

(Euphagus carolinus)

On November 7, 1820, while Audubon was journeying by flatboat from Cincinnati to Natchez, the captain of the boat, Jacob Aumack, shot a male of this species. "As these birds are scarce," Audubon wrote in his journal, "I intend Drawing it tomorrow." The specimen Aumack shot is doubtless the bird at center in this drawing. Both this bird and the one below it, a female, were cut out and pasted down on the paper, to which Audubon added, in 1829, the two young birds at top. Havell completed the composition following Audubon's pencil outlines. The tree is a black-haw *(Viburnum prunifolium)*.

Havell CLVII

PLATE 178

BLACK OYSTERCATCHER
(Haematopus bachmani)

These specimens were sent to Audubon by Dr. John Kirk Townsend and were probably painted in London in 1838. Havell provided a landscape in his engraving. Havell CCCCXXVII

PLATE 179

SCARLET IBIS
(Eudocimus ruber)

These birds, an adult at left and a young ibis at right, were drawn from specimens collected outside the United States. "I have not met," Audubon wrote of the species, "with more than three individuals in a state of liberty, in the whole range of the United States." Although Audubon insisted that he "saw them sufficiently well to be assured of their belonging to the present species," he may have mistaken spoonbills for this South American bird. The painting was probably done in England about 1837. A background was added to the Havell plate. Havell CCCXCVII

PLATE 180

RED-EYED VIREO
(Vireo olivaceus)

"Few birds seem to enjoy life more than this Vireo," Audubon observed, "for at almost every short cessation of its song, it is seen making a movement or two up or along a branch, searching with extreme diligence for food, peeping cautiously under the leaves, and examining each bud or blossom with a care peculiarly its own." The composition was probably completed in Louisiana or Mississippi in 1822. The painstaking detail in the rendering of the spider, its web, and the limb of the honey-locust *(Gleditsia triacanthos)* indicates the work of Joseph Mason.   Havell CL

No 15. Plate 74.
Published
1829.

PLATE 181

IVORY-BILLED WOODPECKER

(Campephilus principalis)

Audubon showed this male, at left, and two females tearing the bark from a dead tree branch to reach the insects beneath. Done before 1826, the painting is inscribed "Louisianna." The vertical line running from the head of the female at lower right is a stain in the paper—one of the few instances of damage in these original paintings. "I have always imagined," Audubon wrote, "that in the plumage of the beautiful Ivory-billed Woodpecker, there is something very closely allied to the style of colouring of the great Vandyke." Frequently observed and affectionately described by Audubon, this species is now probably extinct. It was estimated in 1939 that twenty-two of these woodpeckers survived in the Southeast. Since that time the forest habitats of the birds have been destroyed, leaving them without refuge.   Havell LXVI

Ivory-billed Woodpecker. *Male & Female.*
Picus principalis.—

PLATE 182

LONG-BILLED CURLEW

(Numenius americanus)

This painting was done in late October, 1831, shortly after Audubon and
George Lehman arrived in Charleston. A view of that city, by Lehman,
appears in the background (the spot at lower left is spilled paint). The
artists had received an unexpectedly warm welcome from the Charles-
tonians, especially from the Reverend John Bachman, who insisted that
they stay in his home. In his text Audubon described at length a memor-
able expedition to the "Bird Banks" south of Charleston where he saw
great flocks of long-billed curlews. The day ended with an outdoor feast
at which the artist turned chef. The menu was: "Fish, fowl, and oysters,"
procured on the spot, and "some steaks of beef, and a sufficiency of good
beverage." They had forgotten salt, "but I soon proved to my merry companions that hunters can find a good substitute in their powder-flasks. Our
salt . . . was gunpowder, as it has been with me many a time; and to our
keen appetites, the steaks thus salted were quite as savoury as any . . .
cooked at home."   Havell CCXXXI

PLATE 183

BULLOCK'S ORIOLE
(Icterus bullockii)

BALTIMORE ORIOLE
(Icterus galbula)

NORTHERN WATERTHRUSH
(Seiurus noveboracensis)

VARIED THRUSH
(Ixoreus naevius)

LESSER GOLDFINCH
(Spinus psaltria)

This potpourri of birds was rearranged in Havell's engraving: there, the bird perched on the rock, a northern waterthrush, was placed at the bottom, with the other species ranged above on a tree branch. The topmost bird, a female Bullock's oriole, and the bird just below it, a male of the same species, were collected on June 21, 1836, by Dr. Townsend on the Columbia River in Oregon. (Another male Bullock's oriole appears in Plate 266.) The bird at right, second from the top, is a female Baltimore oriole. (Others of its species are given in Plate 96.) The large bird is a varied thrush; beneath it, in handwriting that is not Audubon's, is inscribed "6. Female Varried Robbin. !introduce it in small plate." Possibly written by Audubon's son John, the inscription may refer to the smaller, octavo edition of *The Birds of America,* published in 1840–44. The pair of lesser goldfinches (a female above, a male below) was drawn from skins lent to Audubon by William Swainson; a male of this species is also included in Plate 280. Havell CCCCXXXIII

PLATE 184

SPARROW HAWK

(Falco sparverius)

In his text Audubon speaks affectionately, and at some length, about a sparrow hawk he once adopted as a pet. "To the last," Audubon wrote, "he continued kind to me, and never failed to return at night to his favourite roost behind the window-shutter. His courageous disposition often amused the family, as he would sail off from his stand, and fall on the back of a tame duck, which, setting up a loud quack, would waddle off in great alarm with the Hawk sticking to her." One of Audubon's biographers has asserted that this bird served as a model for one of the figures in this water color, but the assertion cannot be substantiated. The female hawk is holding a sparrow. The two hawks below are males. Audubon did the painting in the East in 1829, and the birds are shown in a common eastern tree, the butternut *(Juglans cinerea)*. Havell CXLII

PLATE 185 *(overleaf)*

COMMON EIDER

(Somateria mollissima)

"The history of this remarkable duck must ever be looked upon with great interest by the student of nature," Audubon wrote. "The depressed form of its body, the singular shape of its bill, the beautiful colouring of its plumage, the value of its down as an article of commerce, and the nature of its haunts, render it a very remarkable species." Audubon may have drawn these eiders, with the female in the background and two white-backed males in the foreground, near Eastport, Maine, in May of 1833. "I have represented three of these birds in a state of irritation. A mated pair, having a few eggs already laid, have been approached by a single male, and are in the act of driving off the intruder, who, to facilitate his retreat, is lashing his antagonists with his wings." Havell CCXLVI

Barred Owl *Male adult*
Strix nebulosa.—
Grey Squirrel.
Sciurus cinereus.—

PLATE 189

BLACK TERN

(Chlidonias niger)

Audubon probably painted these terns, in winter plumage above and in breeding plumage below, in England about 1835. He may have copied the lower figure from an earlier drawing, done in Kentucky, of the same species. Alexander Wilson, Audubon noted with some satisfaction, "to whom I shewed the old nests of the Black Tern at [a pond in Kentucky], did not seem to be acquainted with the bird, and thought that they were those of some species of Rail."   Havell CCLXXX

PLATE 190

ORANGE-CROWNED WARBLER

(Vermivora celata)

In February of 1832 Audubon and George Lehman were in eastern Florida, where they collaborated on this painting. In autumn, Audubon
reported in his text, this warbler "nearly loses the orange spot" that is
discernible on the head of the lower bird. Lehman painted the sparkle-
berry *(Vaccinium arboreum)*.   Havell CLXXVIII

PLATE 191

LEACH'S PETREL

(Oceanodroma leucorhoa)

Audubon made a sketch of these petrels while on board the packet ship *Columbia,* off the shore of Newfoundland in late August of 1831. This finished drawing was probably done several years later.   Havell CCLX

PLATE 192

KNOT

(Calidris canutus)

Audubon made this composition in Louisiana about 1821. The knot with the reddish breast is in breeding plumage. The other bird, which was cut out and pasted onto the foreground, is in winter plumage. When Havell made his engraving, he eliminated the sailing ship and calmed the seas.

Havell CCCXV

Forked Tail Sea Swallow – Wallorh Stormy Petrel – Leachie Storm...

Red breasted Sandpiper. 1 Male Spring plumage
Tringa islandica, L.   2 Female in Winter.

A. Holmes

1 Spring plumage
2 Winter plumage –

Rocky Mountain Plover
Charadrius Montana
Townsend

Rocky Mountains
female June 1. 1834
I.K. Townsend

Length of foot 2 3/4 inches 12/[...]
3 inches very bristly [...]
with dull soft color

[...] primary length [...] of [...]
[...] color - under [...]
[...]
[...] & foot [...]
[...] beyond the tail. [...]
[...] tail 2 [...]
J.[...]

Nº 70.
Plate 380.

Rocky Mountain Plover.
Charadrius montana. Townsend.
Adult Female. —

PLATE 200

LOUISIANA WATERTHRUSH

(Seiurus motacilla)

"I have taken the liberty of naming this first songster of our groves," Audubon wrote, "after the country which has afforded me my greatest pleasures. . . ." The painting is inscribed "Drawn from Nature by J. J. Audubon Bayou Sarah Louisiana Sepr 27th 1821." The Jack-in-the-pulpit (*Arisaema triphyllum*) was provided by Joseph Mason.   Havell XIX

Louisiana Water Thrush
Turdus ludovicianus

Drawn from Nature by J.J. Audubon
Bayou Sarah Louisiana Feb. 27th 1821

PLATE 201

SNOW BUNTING

(Plectrophenax nivalis)

Audubon sent this water color of two adults (above) and one young snow
bunting (below) to London in March of 1833. He had probably painted
the birds in Boston during that winter, possibly assisted by his younger
son, John. All three of the birds are in winter plumage. In his text Audubon
wrote, "As soon as the cold blasts of winter have stiffened the earth's surface, and brought with them the first snow-clouds, millions of these birds,
driven before the pitiless storm, make their way towards milder climes.
Their wings seem scarcely able to support their exhausted, nay almost con-
gealed bodies, which seem little larger than the great feathery flakes of
the substance from which [the snow buntings] have borrowed their name."

Havell CLXXXIX

PLATE 202 *(overleaf)*

REDDISH EGRET

(Dichromanassa rufescens)

When Audubon first saw these birds in the Florida Keys he was puzzled
by their coloration: "Some of them were as white as driven snow, the rest
of a delicate purplish tint, inclining to grey on the back and wings, with
heads and necks of a curious reddish colour. Males and females there were,
but they were all of one species. . . ." He concluded—incorrectly—that
those with white plumage were immature birds. In this species, coloring
depends on the individual and has no relation to either age or sex. The
egrets illustrated here are both adults. Audubon drew both the birds and
the background in April, 1832, in Florida.   Havell CCLVI

PLATE 203

WARBLING VIREO
(Vireo gilvus)

This painting is inscribed "New Jersey May 23ᵈ." The year was undoubtedly 1829, at which time Audubon was in Camden, New Jersey. He had the rare opportunity, during his stay in Camden, of watching a pair of these vireos build a nest in a poplar tree just outside the window of his lodgings, and he observed the activities of the birds until their offspring hatched and finally flew from the nest. "I bade them adieu at last with great regret," he wrote. In this drawing, the birds are perched in a laurel magnolia tree *(Magnolia virginiana)*.   Havell CXVIII

Warbling Flycatcher.
male 1. F. 2.
Vireo gilvus.

New Jersey may 23.
J. V. A

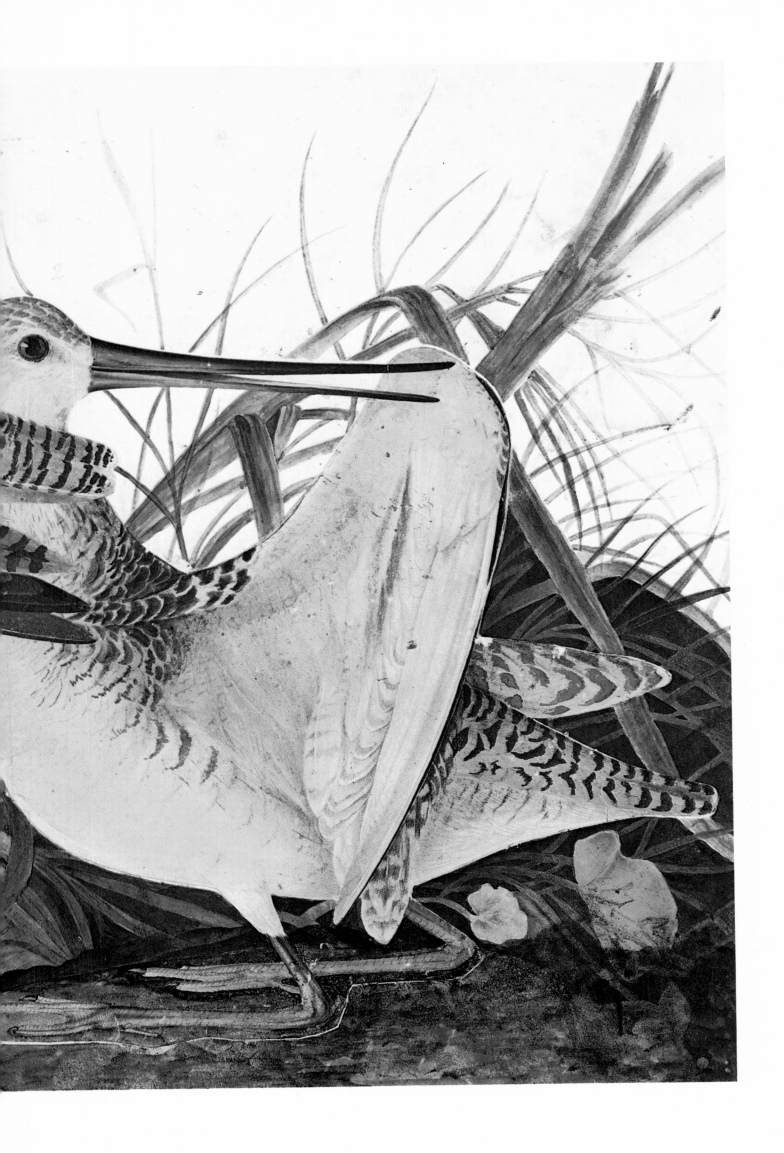

PLATE 210

GULL-BILLED TERN

(Gelochelidon nilotica)

On August 14, 1837, Audubon wrote anxiously from London to John Bachman: "After *Ten Years* or more of constant exertions to obtain, and to study both a good representation, and the *Habits* of our *Marsh Tern,* and when as I thought both were actually in my possession, I find on the opening of all our trunks, boxes, &c that *My Drawing* of this Curiously interesting species is actually *Wanting* or *Missing!* This is the 15th of August, and on the last day of the present year My Work will be finished, but unless you find that Drawing at your House and send it to me immediatly . . . it will come too late." Fortunately, the drawing was found and sent to Audubon. He had painted this tern, in spring plumage, in April of 1837 in the Mississippi River delta. "Excepting the Cayenne Tern," he wrote in his text, "I know no American species that has so powerful a flight as the present. To this power is added an elegant lightness that renders it most conspicuous and pleasing during the love season. Then 'the happy pair' are seen to rise in elegant circling sweeps . . . and only a few feet apart, until they attain a height of about two hundred yards, when they come close together, and then glide with extended pinions through the air . . . both emitting tender and plaintive notes. . . ." Faintly indicated in pencil, the insect that the tern is pursuing was completed in Havell's engraving.   Havell CCCCX

Marsh Tern. *Sterna anglica*

PLATE 211

PINE WARBLER

(Dendroica pinus)

Audubon inscribed this drawing, in ink, "James Pirrie's Plantation Louisi-anna July 10th 1821—Plant J. R. Mason." He considered this warbler a new species (as he had believed the pine warbler in Plate 23 to be undis-covered), and it was not until some time after this painting was made that he learned that Wilson had already recorded the bird. In this paint-ing, a female, above, and a male, below, are perched on a loblolly pine *(Pinus taeda)*.   Havell CXL

Pine Creeping Warbler. Male & female
Sylvia Pinus

Drawn from Nature by John J. Audubon
Louis Pirrie's Plantation Louisiana July 10th 1821

Plate J. R. Mason

PLATE 212

WATER PIPIT

(Anthus spinoletta)

Audubon correctly identified this pipit when he wrote the text to accompany his other drawing of the species (Plate 58). Yet, for some reason, he believed this adult pipit to be a new species, which he named "prairie titlark." He used pencil, pastel, and water color to make this rendering in 1815. The moss phlox *(Phlox subulata)* was probably added to the painting some years later. Havell LXXX

PLATE 213

FOX SPARROW

(Passerella iliaca)

Audubon probably painted these birds in the East in 1824. A variety of woodland plants are shown in the painting, including the partridge-berry *(Mitchella repens)*, with its small white flowers and red berries, and the Christmas fern *(Polystichum acrostichoides)* at right. Havell CVIII

No 16. Plate 80 —
Published 1830 —

ogeus
Phlox Subulata

Pl. 186.

PLATE 223

CAROLINA PARAKEET

(Conuropsis carolinensis)

Done in Louisiana about 1825, this exceptional painting was inscribed at
lower right: "The upper Specimen was shot near Bayou Sarah and appeared
so uncommon having 14 Tail feathers all 7 sizes distinct and firmly affixed
in 14 diferent recepticals that I drew it more to verify one of those aston-
ishing fits of Nature than any thing else—it was a female—The Green
headed [a young bird] is also a singular although not so uncommon a
Variety as the above one—Louisianna—December—J. J. Audubon."
"Doubtless," Audubon wrote in his text, "the reader will say, while look-
ing at the seven figures of Parakeets represented in the plate, that I spared
not my labour. I never do, so anxious am I to promote his pleasure. These
birds are represented feeding on the plant commonly named the *Cockle-
bur* [cocklebur, *Xanthium strumarium*]. . . . Nature seems to have im-
planted in these birds a propensity to destroy, in consequence of which
they cut to atoms pieces of wood, books, and, in short, everything that
comes in their way. . . . The woods are the habitation best fitted for them,
and there the richness of their plumage, their beautiful mode of flight,
and even their screams, afford welcome intimation that our darkest forests and most sequestered swamps are not destitute of charms." Even in
Audubon's day, as he reported, this exquisite bird was a declining species.
Slaughtered by man, caught and caged as pets, they were soon extermi-
nated. In September of 1914, the last surviving Carolina parakeet died in
the Cincinnati Zoological Gardens.   Havell XXVI